Rewired,
Rehired,
or Retired?

Rewired, Rehired, or Retired?

A Global Guide for the Experienced Worker

Robert K. Critchley

JOSSEY-BASS/PFEIFFER
A Wiley Company
www.pfeiffer.com

Published by

JOSSEY-BASS/PFEIFFER
A Wiley Company
989 Market Street
San Francisco, CA 94103-1741
415.433.1740; Fax 415.433.0499
800.274.4434; Fax 800.569.0443

www.pfeiffer.com

ISBN: 0-7879-6219-8

Library of Congress Cataloging-in-Publication Data

Critchley, Robert K.
    Rewired, rehired, or retired? a global guide for the experienced worker /
Robert K. Critchley.
        p. cm.
    ISBN 0-7879-6219-8 (alk. paper)
    1. Retirees—Employment. 2. Job hunting I. Title.
HD6279 .C75 2001
650.14—dc21   2001006601

Printed in the United States of America.

We at Jossey-Bass strive to use the most environmentally sensitive paper stocks available
to us. Our publications are printed on acid-free recycled stock whenever possible, and our
paper always meets or exceeds minimum GPO and EPA requirements.

Acquiring Editor: Josh Blatter
Director of Development: Kathleen Dolan Davies
Developmental Editor: Susan Rachmeler
Editor: Beverly Miller
Senior Production Editor: Dawn Kilgore
Manufacturing Supervisor: Becky Carreño
Cover Design: Bruce Lundquist
Illustrations: Lotus Art

Printing   10 9 8 7 6 5 4 3 2

To dear Merilyn, Jodi, and Shari, who give my life purpose and have always encouraged my every endeavor without judgment

CONTENTS

ACKNOWLEDGMENTS

Many wonderful people contributed to make this book possible and in the process helped me understand better why all of us can achieve dreams. Having often contemplated writing a book such as this in the past, I have created this book by pursuing my long-term dream and overcoming all perceived barriers.

It was over dinner in a favorite restaurant in Sydney with my daughter and son-in-law, Jodi and Brad Storey, that the concept of this book emerged. After much urging, discussing, harassing, and encouraging by Jodi and Brad that night, I decided to start the engines rolling.

Discovery always continues in life if you seek new horizons, and Jodi made an enormous contribution through her superb research and writing skills, translating this book from a recitation about life experiences into an exciting resource. She is extremely creative, and as we put this book together, my respect for her talent, creativity, and persistence grew. This is a classic case of the experienced, mature worker learning from the younger worker. I thank her for her great work.

Writing this book has been a family experience. My wife, Merilyn, gave me constant support by providing me with valuable feedback, observations, and suggestions for case studies and encouraging me to continue in spite of other work pressures, even if it meant that she saw less of me.

My daughter, Shari Fryer, who lives in the United States, made an incredible contribution by providing international research and content suggestions. In particular, she challenged me when my message was not clear or consistent. Her continuing enthusiasm and support throughout this whole journey were inspiring.

Shari was also instrumental in introducing me to the amazingly talented, ever youthful, creative genius Maureen Sullivan of DBM Publishing. Maureen immediately became passionate about the book and its goal to lift the quality of people's lives (and in fact, after intense brainstorming, it was Maureen who came up with the title of this book). Her enthusiasm for the task was so infectious that if I ever had doubts about completing the book, I knew I couldn't let her down. Maureen introduced me to Josh Blatter, the editor at Jossey-Bass who liked the concept, and from there this book became a reality.

I am grateful to Gerald Purgay, senior vice president of marketing at DBM, and Tom Silveri, president and CEO of DBM, for their support and encouragement.

Thanks to Tim Lynch who provided much guidance and support on content, structure, and presentation, as well as ensuring that the book would have a global appeal. He has been a pleasure to work with. Also, thanks to Shane Stewart for his contribution and friendship.

Lyn Tarbuck, my extremely professional secretary, has been of great assistance in helping track down sources and information from DBM around the world. I deeply appreciate her tireless efforts, professionalism, and tolerance.

Many of my friends at DBM provided valuable input, research, and feedback. I particularly thank Vicky Bloch (president, DBM Brazil), Lesley Elliot (DBM New Zealand), Edgardo Loret de Mola (DBM Peru), and Sidney Simkin (DBM United Kingdom) for their valuable contributions.

I express a huge thank-you to my international colleagues who responded to my request for information on the situations of experienced workers in their countries. These people include (in no particular order) Marcus Herold, Jacques Eliard, Ines Temple, Tomas Silva, Kyu Kim, Tad Otsuki, Jacques Feron, Neil McDonald, Larry Cambron, Dora Wong, Karen Russell, Leigh Scott-Kemmis, Melva Daley Smith, Denis St. Amour, John Gilkes, Deanie Sultana, Barbara Kempster, Linda Neville, and Takako Yanase.

I would also like to acknowledge the great work undertaken by everyone at my publisher, Jossey-Bass. The team was thoroughly professional and supportive every step of the way, and I am extremely appreciative. In particular, thanks to Susan Rachmeler for being so kind with feedback on the manuscript and for her valuable suggestions, and thanks to Josh Blatter, Kathleen Dolan Davies, Jeanenne Ray, Jesica Church, Dawn Kilgore, and Beverly Miller for their support.

I especially express my gratitude to the many DBM clients on outplacement programs who gave me such rich anecdotes and wonderful stories to share. They helped me appreciate how we can all make a difference to our own and other people's lives.

I hope I haven't forgotten anyone, but if I have, please forgive me.

FOREWORD

The largest segment of the world population is that of the aging baby boomer. And as my friend and colleague Bob Critchley goes to press with *Rewired, Rehired, or Retired?* the offspring of the greatest generation are facing a retirement options menu never dreamed possible by their parents.

The mothers and fathers of baby boomers spent between twenty-five and forty years at a company that recruited, developed, nurtured, and planned for the retirements of its employees. The end of work was usually at the age of sixty-five, complete with a party and a gold watch, and followed by a quiet retirement playing golf and hide-and-seek with the grandchildren.

A lot has changed since then.

Baby boomers, the first generation to take their careers into their own hands, are at the edge of another new frontier. They now need to learn how to take charge of their "retirement" and will benefit from the possibilities featured in this book.

As international president for Drake Beam Morin, Critchley's finger is on the global pulse when it comes to the subject of careers and mature workers. His reach stretches into the working populations of forty-three countries, and his experience coaching and inspiring spans better than twenty years. He knows his subject cold.

Whether you find yourself tired of being retired, in transition due to downsizing, or wishing to reinvent yourself in the next iteration of your work life, the thought-provoking and creative suggestions in this book will help you plan an appealing and exciting next chapter that will both satisfy and fulfill.

Whether you're a human resource director whose sphere of influence affects the lives of baby boomers or a baby boomer yourself, *Rewired, Rehired, or Retired?* is must reading on a most important subject.

Tom Silveri
CEO and President
Drake Beam Morin, Inc.

PREFACE
Lead Your Life, Don't Follow It!

If you are approaching or have reached or passed your fiftieth birthday and if there are times when you wonder about the future and think about what you should or could be doing with your career and your life, then this book is for you.

If your days are marked by full enjoyment and complete satisfaction, then congratulations. Count your blessings, carry on, and share your learnings with others. But if you ever find yourself wondering whether life has taken you in directions that haven't entirely met your needs or completely fulfilled your dreams, then read on. And remember the phrase, "life has taken you," because the point of this book is to convince you that as you've matured, you've gained the skills, resources, experience, and understanding to lead your life, not just follow it.

Most of us are blessed to live in free societies that offer abundant career and life choices. We can look at the world with fresh eyes and realize that our choices are almost certainly greater than we have ever imagined. But to take advantage of the opportunities, we may need to eliminate real or imagined barriers that get in our way.

Your life is unique, and you need to decide what is right for you. This book is designed to inspire—and even provoke—you to think seriously about what you are doing today and where you are headed—to plan and then take action.

I offer my own career experience as a good example of the difference between leading a life and following it, because I have done both. I grew up in a small town in Australia, where my father left a secure job working for the railways to open a café and newspaper store with my mother. At the time, children were often expected to start work at a young age, and my older brother and I were not exceptions to that rule. Starting at age nine, I climbed out of bed seven days a week at 4:00 A.M. to prepare newspapers for distribution and then help deliver them around the town. After school, I sold more papers to people in the street, at local hotels, and at local businesses and worked in my parents' store too.

My parents always assumed that given its size and prospects, the family business could support one, but not two, of their children for the long term, and my older brother continued on with it. Lacking any real plans or career aspirations, I joined the local branch of a national bank when I left school at age sixteen. At the outset, my responsibilities did not qualify as high finance: I chopped firewood and filled inkwells. Still, my parents were pleased with my employment, because in those days, working in a bank meant security. And when my employer realized that I was good with numbers, I began to be promoted up the ranks. Before long, I had moved on from my hometown to work in large cities in Australia and then around the world.

But as I continued to advance in my profession, I discovered that banking did not particularly excite me. It allowed me to pursue my studies and complete my education, and I gained worldwide experience in a rapidly developing industry. But I often wondered whether I was just doing what was expected of me, pulled along by pride in my accomplishments at the bank and comforted by the prospects of ongoing job security, increasing prosperity, and, finally, a comfortable retirement.

I grew bored and realized I wanted new challenges and additional stimulation in my career and life. I imagined what it would be like to do something different but avoided exploring new career avenues. I even found myself wishing for a calamity that would force me in a new direction.

I got my wish in a sudden and tragic way when my father died unexpectedly. Although he had always been incredibly supportive and loving and was never overbearing or overpowering, I realized that perhaps the main reason I had continued to work hard at the bank was that he and my other relatives had felt so proud of me. But I also realized that as much as I didn't want to upset those closest to me, this was my life and I should not be living it to please anyone else. It was time to be honest with myself and pursue my own goals.

Three days after my father's death, when I was forty-one years old and had spent twenty-five years in the banking industry, and after some long discussions with my wife and two daughters, I resigned from my senior management role to start my own consulting business.

My company grew from small beginnings, but it grew successfully as I took the skills and experience I had developed in banking and applied them to companies and people in other industries. The real key was that I was now doing something I felt truly passionate about.

I developed my team to create strategic plans for companies and helped others recover from financial crisis and improve their profitability. I achieved greater work satisfaction in my professional life and greater peace within myself knowing that for the first time in my career, I was making a real difference in the quality of people's lives.

The experience I gained in my consulting business revealed other areas where my skills and experience were relevant. Subsequently, my colleagues and I founded an outplacement business in Australia under a license from Drake Beam Morin Inc (DBM), the world's largest outplacement and career management company. I realized that I had now moved to a truly exciting career where I could continue to make a difference to people's lives. My colleagues and I built the business into a successful national operation, ultimately selling it to DBM Inc., where I now serve in a senior global role.

This book is certainly not about my life. I share my experiences only to show how an unexpected event or personal decision can change the trend and purpose of one's life and to demonstrate that the skills and experience we all possess can be applied in a variety of areas. I have successfully transferred my skills among the three main industries I have worked in: finance, professional consulting services, and career transition.

If you take a hard and honest look at your life, examining the twists and turns it has taken, you might decide to do something completely different. Or you could find that you really do enjoy the things you are doing today and continue on with them. Whatever your decision, you will feel more confident, because you will have thought through the range of options that can help you achieve a rewarding and satisfying future.

You may not have a choice, of course. With rampant merger and acquisition activity, periods of economic turmoil in different parts of the world, and an intense focus on increased productivity and improved performance, can anyone feel truly secure in a job or career today? There may be a few people left in some corner of the world who anticipate starting a job straight from school or college with the expectation that they will stay with the same employer until they retire. That is probably a very risky assumption.

The sobering—but ultimately empowering—fact of the matter is that in this ever-changing world, the only person who can be responsible for your career is you. Loyalty and hard work no longer guarantee stability. Employers no longer take responsibility for your career or even guarantee you'll have a job in a year's time. How can they, when they can no longer be sure that they will exist in the future?

Losing a job can be a daunting experience, of course, particularly if you are attempting to reenter the marketplace after years of secure employment. Should this be your situation, this book can help you reduce trauma and stress, turning your transition period into an opportunity to initiate choices for a far more enjoyable future.

The good news is how amazingly the world of work has developed in the past fifty years. New opportunities make employment more meaningful than meaningless. Retirement once meant preparing for death; now it signals the start of a new phase in an exciting life. Life expectancy has grown dramatically. At the age of fifty today, you have every reason to think about what you will be doing for the next twenty to forty years or more. As long as health permits, you don't have to sell your house and move to a retirement village, unless that is honestly what you and those close to you want to do.

I believe I have one of the best jobs imaginable, working with individuals around the world who are going through career transition. I gather and share experiences and strategies that have worked for others. When I visit a DBM office, I spend time with people working on job search, encouraging them to focus clearly on their ultimate career and life goals to help them move successfully forward. Rich with success stories that have worked for other people, I find that my workdays are an ongoing journey of discovery and self-discovery.

Throughout this book, I have combined personal experience with the experience of others who have gone through transition in their lives. These stories will help you take on the challenges of your own life, enabling you to move forward with a strong sense of purpose, direction, motivation, satisfaction, and, most important, peace within yourself.

The choices you face may include these:

- Continuing to work hard in your current job—or in a new position— to achieve further career goals, because you enjoy your work and gain great satisfaction from it

- Maintaining your working life at a steady and enjoyable pace but without working long hours, allowing you time to pursue other interests

- Deciding to stop working completely or to work part time in order to devote more time to other options and interests

In this book, we will explore these three options—and the gray areas between them—in a nonjudgmental way. Remember that whatever direction you choose is fine, as long as you have considered your options vigorously and worked out the path that is best for you. If you decide to continue in or rejoin the workforce, this book will give you many good suggestions, enabling you to gain a competitive advantage in the job market.

Whatever your age, the next chapter of your life starts right now. Whether you are rich or poor, happily employed, retired, recently terminated, or frustrated in a boring or meaningless job, you have a precious opportunity to rethink your life and what you will do with the rest of it.

It will not all be plain sailing. But it is my fervent hope that the experiences and suggestions set out in this book will help make the journey smoother and more enriching for you.

Rewired,
Rehired,
or Retired?

CHAPTER 1

Achieving a Work-Life Balance

He who is not courageous enough to take risks will accomplish nothing in life.
Muhammad Ali (1942–), world champion heavyweight boxer

Do you remember a time in your life, perhaps long ago in your youth, when your heart was full of dreams and aspirations for the future? Are those feelings only a distant memory, or have you maintained an active focus over the years to seek and attain your goals in your professional and personal life?

THE FUTURE STARTS TODAY

Life is not a dress rehearsal. Now—*right now*—is the time to get serious (and also adventurous and excited) and take the necessary steps to create and nurture the purposeful future you may have wished for, but may also have neglected working toward.

Remember that your future is precisely that: yours and yours alone. You are the only one who can make the right decisions for the rest of your life by examining your accomplishments, needs, values, and goals closely and then acting on them. You will certainly want to consult with and be considerate of the needs and goals of the people around you who are important in your life. But ultimately, as I learned when I made the move from banking to consulting in my own career, your career is your responsibility.

All of us are unique in terms of our ability to cope with change, face new challenges, and make good and meaningful decisions. As mature individuals, we have accumulated wide-ranging experiences throughout our lives, both professionally and personally. By examining and assessing all the knowledge that experience provides us, we possess the necessary resources to make effective decisions about the future.

> *If your success is not on your own terms, if it looks good to the world but does not feel good in your heart, it is not success at all.*
>
> Anna Quindlen, author

It can be difficult, however, to assimilate this information, standing back from the day-to-day world, and determining a proper course for the future. This chapter will help you chart that course.

Case Study: A Matter of Personal Choice

Fred recently turned fifty-seven years old. He had left school at a young age to take a job in a local bank branch. He worked hard and was promoted rapidly through the ranks of the bank and undertook additional studies to further his career.

Fred's career continued to advance, which resulted in a good standard of living for him and his family. He managed to avoid any dramatic changes in his life on the road to prosperity, career development, raising a family, and building assets. Fred has now achieved financial security in the way of savings, equity in his home, and other investments. His children have been well educated and have moved away from home to live their lives independently.

Over the past thirty or so years, Fred has worked for several organizations but has always been extremely focused on working hard to achieve and maintain a decent standard of living for his family. His focus on

Rewired, Rehired, or Retired?

leisure activities throughout this time has been limited to annual vacations and some athletic pursuits.

Fred's employer has recently undergone a number of internal structural changes due to a recent takeover. As a result, Fred recognizes the possibility of losing his job. He is faced with the need to contemplate his future and his eventual retirement.

Fred thinks in terms of three primary considerations:

- Remain active and continue to develop in the corporate world to pursue greater achievements for as long as he is physically and mentally capable.
- Maintain the traditional career path of working through to age sixty-five or thereabouts and then move into retirement.
- Retire early in the event of a forced retirement.

The key for Fred is to pursue the path that will be most fulfilling for him personally. His challenge is to decide on the most desirable option, which will allow him to achieve and maintain his ideal work-life balance. Only he, with the support of his wife, can decide what is right for him at this stage in his life. Fred's decision is unique and very personal.

WHAT ARE YOUR CHOICES?

As Fred has learned, determining the right choice for your future can usually be narrowed down to three choices:

1. Continue to work hard to achieve further career goals because you enjoy your work and gain great satisfaction from what you are doing. If others brand you a workaholic, so what? It's your life, and if you're enjoying it and have a sense of achievement and are maintaining good health, that's fine. Do be sure, however, to give yourself regular breaks to recharge your batteries and pursue other interests away from work. A better term for you, because you enjoy what you do, may be a *workaphile.*

2. Maintain your working life at a steady, enjoyable pace, without working long hours. This choice allows time for personal and social interests on a regular basis in the context of a routine work life with regular hours. If

others suggest that you ought to be working harder, so what? It's your life. You may plan to continue in this vein until your normal retirement date.

3. Decide to stop working. If you don't enjoy your work role and have reached the point where you have some financial security, you may want to say good-bye to work. If others say you're too young to retire, so what? It's your life. You may have hobbies and other pursuits that you want to enjoy. You may simply want to take life a little easier.

Which is the right course of action for you? All are good choices. There are no right or wrong answers, as long as you have thought through the alternatives and decided which one is right for you. The key is to be satisfied that you will enjoy what you do and will be pleasing yourself, not satisfying other people's wishes.

Note, however, that the first two broad options, which focus on continuing your career, are not necessarily tied to your current job or even the industry or area in which you work today. It *is* possible to start a new career at age fifty, sixty, or any other age, for that matter, if you realize that making a change will reinvigorate you personally as well as professionally.

BETTER HEALTH + LONGER LIFE = MORE CHOICES

Today, most people enjoy better health than at any other time in the world's history, possess greater financial resources, and have broader retirement options, including the choice to retire at a later age or—at least in the traditional sense of retirement—not at all.

One of the most significant changes in recent history is the continuing increase in life expectancy. Advances in medicine and health practices have helped double the average life span of Americans in the past two hundred years (Butler, 2000). Life spans vary throughout the world, of course, depending on medical advances and services available, environmental conditions, genes, and other factors that determine the range of aging. Still, the maximum attainable life span for humans is currently thought to be in the vicinity of 120 years. This is encouraging and perhaps daunting news: time may no longer be the scarce resource when middle-aged individuals consider their futures.

Making a Choice.

Consider the following questions when determining whether to continue working hard, ease up some, or retire:

- List the three things you enjoy most in your life (work related or nonwork related).

_____

_____

_____

- If you gave up work or reduced your current income, have you adequate funds to enjoy your desired standard of living until you are eighty-five years old?

_____

_____

_____

- Do you have fun each day?

_____

_____

_____

- Do you have good business and personal relationships?

_____

_____

_____

- Do you make a difference in your job?

_____

_____

_____

(Continued)

Making a Choice. (Continued)

- Do you have time to see your friends and family as often as you would like?

_____

_____

_____

_____

- Think what you would like to achieve over the next five years. Have you the time, money, and energy to achieve those goals?

_____

_____

_____

_____

- If you have children or grandchildren, do you spend enough time with them? Remember, with children, you only have a loan of them until they grow up, so don't think you can defer spending time with them for five years.

_____

_____

_____

_____

- If you have a spouse or partner and you changed how you spend each day, what would be the impact on that person?

_____

_____

_____

_____

In the industrialized nations of Western Europe and North America, expanding life spans and contracting birthrates have introduced the well-publicized phenomenon of an aging population. Among the world's larger countries, Italy, for example, stands out as the most "aged" society, with 23 percent of its populace aged sixty or older. Countries in East and Southeast Asia are also aging rapidly. With 22 percent of its population age sixty or older, Japan currently is the "oldest" of all Asian nations (West & Kinsella, 1999).

DEALING WITH STRESS

It is no secret that working too hard can induce stress. What may be less well known is that boredom or a lack of direction in life can also bring on stress.

You may have experienced times in your life when you were bored from being too idle and found yourself focusing far too much on small issues, believing that they were in fact vital issues and had to be addressed urgently. I think we all know friends, relatives, or associates who seem to prefer dwelling on the negatives rather than the positives and spend their time feeling stressed about matters that most of us would deem trivial. This particular type of stress is indeed unhealthy and can be harmful to our well-being.

Be sure to maintain your health and fitness. Often, the fitter we become, the more resilient we are to stressful situations. Those of us who have a competitive spirit and enjoy the challenge of achieving goals, whether at work or play, often experience a type of stress while striving to accomplish these goals. There's no evidence, to my knowledge, that this particular type of stress is unhealthy. But to plan for the future, you need to control the stress you are willing to accept.

> *Don't do things to not die, do things to enjoy living. The by-product may be not dying.*
>
> Bernie S. Siegel,
> American author and lecturer

Identifying the path you want to follow to fulfill your dreams and maintain a satisfying work-life balance can go a long way toward removing stress from your life.

YOU DON'T HAVE TO RETIRE

If you are physically and mentally capable, you don't have to retire at all, regardless of your chronological age. The great news is the traditional rules of retirement no longer apply. If you think that such rules remain in place, now is a good time to break them. I have friends in their seventies who, continuing to balance their life choices, are working full time not because they have to work but because they want to.

Attaining a comfortable financial position is obviously a common goal to provide freedom to pursue different activities and alleviate financial stress and strain. But although there's no denying that it does have its benefits, money is not a goal for everyone. What you need to determine is whether you have the necessary financial resources to live a comfortable life—as you define it—while considering the fact that your life expectancy may be eighty or ninety years or even more.

Hold a vision of life that you want and that vision will become fact.

Norman Vincent Peale
(1898–1993), American Christian
Pastor, author

Once again, this is all a question of what matters to you. How can you achieve your goals and fulfill the balance you desire in both your professional and personal life? Many people have no choice but to continue working because of financial needs, whether to pay the mortgage on their house (or pay rent), to educate their children, or to pay off debts.

But many other people, particularly those over age fifty who have worked hard over the years, have significant financial resources: retirement funds, investments, and an accumulation of assets that provide them with the freedom of choice. Financial well-being is not reflected by a hard and fast number, of course. For many, if not most of us, extreme wealth is not a prerequisite for a sense of personal and financial satisfaction. Additional earnings may not dramatically add to the true quality of your life.

So how do you make an effective choice between continuing to work or retiring? On the one hand, you can assess whether the benefits of continued employment are worth the pressures that may accompany them: extensive business travel requirements, keeping up with changing technology, constant decision making, or ongoing performance pressures, for example. Even if you feel that continuing to work makes the most sense for you, it may still be wise to ask, "Why?" Do you want to keep working for your own well-being? For your family? To create a wonderful inheritance for your children? If your reasons seem to have less to do with your own priorities and more with the needs of others, you might want to reexamine them.

Suppose, on the other hand, that retirement is something you're anticipating. What does it mean to you? Have you been longing for the day where you can throw your corporate responsibilities out the window to pursue a life of golfing, reading, and vacationing? That's wonderful, and you ought to make a plan that leads directly to retirement.

As with continued employment, however, it may be helpful to check your feelings. Retirement, as it is traditionally defined, is often perceived as an ending and can be associated with boredom, growing old, no longer being useful, or even preparing for death. Although retirement does create more time for leisure, it can lead to high levels of stress and anxiety for people who don't honestly embrace the idea or who are not yet ready to retire. From any point of view, it does indeed signify the end of one chapter in your life and the commencement of another, which will not only be new but exciting.

Most people don't give a lot of thought to how they'll react to retirement. One thing to remember is that you don't have to rush headlong into full retirement. You have choices. Think about them, choose carefully, and plan ahead. The last thing you want is to wake up one morning, find yourself retired, and only then ask yourself, "Okay, now what?"

Even as retirement has ceased to be a forgone conclusion for many of us, another important change has invaded the working world: there is no such thing as lifelong employment and therefore no such thing as a preordained retirement date. Unexpected job loss can make retirement seem like the most attractive option in the short term, but it may not prove to be the best solution once the shock and grief of job loss are overcome.

JOB SECURITY IS ANCIENT HISTORY!

The likelihood of a change in employment is beyond our control. In the United States, the value of merger activity from 1990 to 2000 has increased twelve times (Mergerstat, 2001). Whenever a merger or takeover occurs, no employees, not even those at the top, have absolute job security.

Many people may have started jobs when they left high school or college with the belief that they would stay with the same organization for their working life. They were told, "Do a good job, and the company will look after you." Sound familiar?

In some countries, this belief has continued until recent years. For example, workers in Japan were deemed to be wedded to the company they worked for. This model, however, has suffered an irreversible breakdown, and workers in Japan are now responsible for their own careers rather than relying on the company they work for.

Globalization, demands from investors, and mergers have all led to a new way of work. Total mergers announced in 1997 had a total value of $1.6 trillion. The level of merger activity has continued to grow, with mergers announced around the world in the year 2000 totaling $3.4 trillion (Thomson Financial Services, 2001). This is a doubling of activity level in just three years!

In this new millennium, each of us is responsible for our own career and professional and personal development. Companies can no longer offer employees lifetime job security because they can't guarantee their own existence. We can no longer depend on an employer for future security, career fulfillment, and personal happiness.

Rewired, Rehired, or Retired?

MAINTAINING BALANCE IN THE WORK-LIFE EQUATION

Just how much of your time you devote to work or pleasure is usually dependent on how much you enjoy what you do. Do not, however, fall into the familiar trap of all work and no play.

A year ago, a partner in a very large Sydney legal firm, Allen Allen & Hemsley, was working late one Tuesday night when he should have been on vacation with his family. For reasons unknown—a fit of pique, perhaps—he sent an e-mail to the rest of the office in which he is reported to have said: "Any lawyer who responds, 'I'd like to help, but I've got a lot on' when I approach him or her with work in the next few days will be well-advised to have a good reason why the only people working at 10:30 tonight are me and two senior colleagues."

The e-mail was leaked to the press and did nothing to enhance the firm's reputation.

The "endless-hours syndrome" is now out of fashion. The macho "I-can-work-longer-than-you" fad peaked in the 1990s. That decade yielded many a sad story of workplace stress. A few avoided burnout by cutting up their credit cards and running away to rear goats.

Workers in the 1990s, whether at the bottom, middle, or top of the ladder, felt powerless. Downsizing was in fashion and there was fat that needed to be trimmed. But some chief executive officers, who stood to reap huge rewards if their company's share price headed due north, ached to get their hands on the check and went on a firing frenzy. Other top management, even if they felt staff cuts were not truly necessary, developed a compulsion to slim employee roles just in case a competitor looked leaner and therefore more attractive.

Since the notorious e-mail, the law firm has invested in a new director of human resources, Ann Kenna, and she has set about changing the culture. She is proud of her first-year results: "The newly completed end-of-year assessment forms show that morale is up by 21 percent, from 38 percent to 59 percent, and that overall satisfaction with the workplace is up from 66 percent to 79 percent."

Law firms may find difficulty heading the best employer list. But accounting firm Deloitte Touche Tohmatsu, with three thousand employees across Australia, had no trouble heading the professional section of Hewitt Associates' survey, Best Companies to Work for in Australia.

Peter May, Deloitte's director of human resources, says that after twenty years in the field, this is the first organization he has worked for where a serious attempt is being made to change the work culture.

Staff are encouraged to draw up personal plans that include a section on how they intend to achieve a work-life balance. Anyone who works excessive hours is likely to be referred for counseling. Staff are recognized for taking hours off to attend key events in their children's lives.

"We want them to enjoy work and have decent lives," says May. "They work better that way. For two years I was on the board of a hospital, which took half a day a month. The firm was very supportive. You can't treat people as industrial goods anymore.

"We have totally flexible hours, which means people come and go at will as long as it doesn't affect their clients."

A handful of the firm's partners work part-time or—in their words—accept a reduced portfolio to fit with other commitments, which could be playing sport for the state—that is, representing their home state in sports competitions—or, more likely, "parental duties."

Linda Christmas, "Knock Off Time," *Weekend Australian,* January 27, 2001.

Rewired, Rehired, or Retired?

Workaholics (or workaphiles) labor incredibly hard and extremely long hours. We may sometimes wonder whether such people have a home to go to, but the fact is that many are focused on work because of the enjoyment it brings them and the satisfaction and stimulation they take from their jobs.

Working hard is fine as long as you get a buzz out of it and as long as the buzz does not come at the expense of your health or life balance. If you are really passionate about working, why punish yourself (and undoubtedly those around you) by retiring? Remember, a workaphile is someone who enjoys working (and it certainly sounds a lot better than a *workaholic*).

You may have a job that gives you great satisfaction and makes you feel you are making a difference. If so, that's wonderful. Still, it makes sense to reassure yourself that you haven't immersed yourself and your life entirely in your job, no matter how enjoyable you may find it.

Deloitte Consulting grasped the nettle in an imaginative way with its Senior Partners Program. It realized that the proportion of its partners over age fifty, when they can retire, would nearly double to 43 percent by 2003. It had to find a way of keeping the best in the firm.

A carefully selected group of eight partners have therefore been invited to dream up their ideal mix of work, leisure, and voluntary activities for the next few years.

One of them is John Everett, former head of the U.K. practice, who hopes to be devoting 40 percent of his working time to a leading arts charity by the end of this year. His advice, which will be free to the charity, will be subsidized by Deloitte, which will continue to pay him on a full-time basis. He will spend 10 percent of his time as a mentor to younger colleagues and the rest as a senior adviser to one or two big clients.

"Financially I was in a position where I could retire," he says. "I enjoy the interaction with clients and with new, younger people in the firm. But there were other things I wanted to do. The alternative would have been to say I'd have to leave the firm to do those things outside."

Many successful people at his age want to make a contribution in both the business and nonbusiness world, but find this difficult to do, he says. "The classic thing is to retire and do a few non-executive things, but that doesn't give you enough involvement to make a difference."

The program, which will add more partners each year, is valuable to the participants and the firm, says Sandy Aird, a senior adviser to Deloitte Consulting and chairman of the selection committee.

Alison Maitland, "The Benefits of Going Gradually,"
Financial Times, August 2, 2000.

To balance your life, you need to set some time aside for outside pursuits that offer you a healthy mix of career and leisure: planning a vacation, taking part in sports or exercise, making travel plans (perhaps starting to plan your next vacation as soon as you return from this one, both to have something exciting to anticipate and to make sure that you don't allow work demands to postpone vacations continually). You may even wish to pursue a lifelong ambition: writing a novel perhaps, or studying a new language or subject. You might want to set some of these goals in conjunction with your spouse, partner, or friends.

What is going to give you the greatest enjoyment and satisfaction? The extremes range from total commitment to work, to total commitment to leisure, to anything and everything between the two extremes. You need to identify the right balance for you.

If you decide you are not sufficiently inspired by your work environment to choose working over retirement, make sure you have a retirement plan in place. People who have always focused their energies on hobbies and family find it easier to take the step into retirement. They can't wait to retire so they can do more of the things they already enjoy.

People who have focused on their careers and worked hard all their lives often find it difficult to switch off. It is not always easy to let go of the past, even a stressful past.

There are many people, for example, who love golf so much that they crave the opportunity to get out on the golf course each day. Golf is their life's passion. If someone would rather be playing golf than working, that's great, as long as the choice really is fulfilling.

Just as in a successful working career, you need to have goals in place to achieve a rewarding and satisfying retirement. If you're that inveterate golfer, for instance, one of your goals might be to reduce your golf handicap. Someone else might want to increase the distance she walks each week to prepare for a future vacation that will demand improved fitness levels. Someone else might want to become involved in community or charitable work. Each can be the perfect choice, as long as it fulfills the individual's goals.

France's shorter working week of thirty-five hours has confounded its critics, producing lower unemployment and happier *travailleurs*.

In Portugal, Stephan remembers working in a publishing company for months at a stretch without a day off. Life wasn't much different for him in Spain either. Now with an executive position in a French publishing company in Paris, he still works hard—but for fifty hours a week rather than ninety. "France is a workers' paradise," he marvels, "and it's such a civilized way to live."

In the next few months, his company must introduce France's astonishingly interventionist experiment in labor regulation: the thirty-five-hour week. Since it became law on January 1, 2000, about 5 million French workers have added an average of fifteen days to their already generous annual leave, effectively pocketing an 11.4 percent wage rise. As a *cadre*, or manager, Stephan's hours will be calculated on an annual basis and he will be required to take off an extra week or two on top of the six-week annual holiday he is already owed.

The thirty-five-hour week was considered an outlandish political stunt when introduced to the 1997 election campaign by Lionel Jospin, the leader of France's Socialist party. Who could seriously believe chronic unemployment—at that time 12.6 percent, or 4 million people—would be eased by paying people their thirty-nine-hour salary for working thirty-five hours? But Jospin was the surprise victor, and brandishing large state subsidies and a small army of *inspecteurs du travail*, his government turned an election slogan into reality within two years.

Analysts and employers predicted catastrophe: already burdened by high taxes and labor costs, French industry would surely become hopelessly uncompetitive, businesses would collapse, unemployment would increase. Even the Left hesitated, wondering whether the workplace agreements required by the thirty-five-hour legislation might undo hard-won rights.

A year later, the critics have been confounded by a remarkable twist of fate: the first year of *les trente-cinq heures* has coincided with 3 percent growth in the French economy, boundless consumer confidence, and unemployment at a nine-year low of 9.2 percent. A recent survey by the American Chamber of Commerce in France found that most U.S. companies operating in France still believed the thirty-five-hour working week was a retrograde step for the nation, but an unanticipated 39 percent of them had created new jobs in response to the law and 20 percent had increased productivity by reorganizing work practices. The law requiring workplace agreements in tandem with the thirty-five-hour week has meant companies can tailor their rosters to meet fluctuations and seasonal changes in demand.

Helen Anderson, "France Finds Time for the Good Life," *Weekend Australian*, January, 27, 2001.

REMAIN ACTIVE AND CONSIDER THE NEEDS OF OTHERS

One retirement option is never a perfect choice or even an acceptable option. It is never healthy to become idle and maintain little or no contact with others. You need to continue to interact with others. If you choose to step away from the workplace, make certain that your planning includes strategies and tactics for living an active life with purposeful activities that will help you avoid boredom—or, worse yet, depression—while preserving a healthy sense of self and self-esteem. Research indicates that interacting with

Rewired, Rehired, or Retired?

others and continuing to learn new skills correlate positively with continued good health.

Don't be afraid your life will end; be afraid that it will never begin.

Grace Hansen

Another important factor to keep in mind regarding your own retirement is that over the years, your spouse or partner may have grown used to being at home alone during the week. Consider how your newly increased presence might affect that daily routine. Will you be considered a nuisance in your own home? Speak openly to your family and friends about the choices you are facing. Share your feelings, and seek feedback from those close to you.

I recently observed a situation where a professional person (let's call him Max) retired and had such a passion for playing golf he decided to move to Hawaii because of the wonderful weather, great golf courses, and the opportunity to play five times a week. (Max is a self-centered man who always wants his own way.)

Although his long-suffering wife (let's call her Jan) had many friends, family, and interests in their home state of Washington, Max insisted on Jan's accompanying him. Jan doesn't play golf, she can't see her grandchildren regularly anymore, and she has no friends in Hawaii. For the past year, she has been miserable. After retiring, Max thought only about himself, with ultimately unpleasant side effects.

YOUR OPTIONS

As you are pondering the most effective future path for achieving your ideal work-life balance, it may help to consider several points:

- If the idea of continued employment appeals to you, what form should it take? Do you want to stay where you are today, seek employment elsewhere, start your own business, or undertake contract or consulting work?

- Does temporary work, and the additional time it offers for leisure activities, seem inviting?

- What can you do to maintain or improve your health and fitness?
- Do you often feel tired and weary? If so, when do you feel the weariest, and when do you feel energetic? Your answer could be an indication of what you enjoy.

He who cannot rest, cannot work; he who cannot let go, cannot hold on; he who cannot find footing, cannot go forward.

Harry Emerson Fosdick
(1878–1969), American minister

- What is your financial status? How much will your retirement cost? Can you cover this without seriously reducing your assets?
- Are you being honest with yourself as you ask and answer tough questions?

SUMMARY

This is not someone else's life you are planning. It is yours! Decide what you want to do that will give you the greatest happiness and satisfaction. You don't want to spend the rest of your life reflecting on what once was. Make the right decisions now, and look forward to new experiences with enthusiasm.

It's up to you to design your future to suit the life you want to live. Remember a few key points:

- *The future starts today.* You're the only one who can make the right decisions for the forthcoming sequence of events in your life by closely examining your accomplishments, needs, competencies, values, and goals.
- *What are your choices?* What is going to give you the greatest enjoyment and satisfaction? Your options range from total commitment to work to total commitment to leisure, and everything in between. You need to identify the right balance for you. Only you can decide.
- *Better health + longer life = More choices.* Retirement options have broadened as health generally has improved and adequate financial resources have become more common.

Rewired, Rehired, or Retired?

- *Dealing with stress.* Boredom or lack of direction in life can cause negative stress. To plan for the future, you need to control the stress you are willing to accept.
- *You don't have to retire.* Retirement may hold no appeal for you. Because life expectancy has increased, the belief that a person is ready for retirement by the age of sixty or sixty-five is now antiquated. The traditional rules of retirement no longer apply. You now have the choice to retire or take an alternate path.
- *Maintaining balance in the work-life equation.* To balance your life, you need to set some time aside for pursuits that offer you a healthy mix of career and leisure.
- *Remain active and consider the needs of others.* If you choose to step down from the workplace, be sure to maintain an active life with purposeful activities. Talk with your family and friends about the choices you are considering. Share your feelings, and seek feedback.
- *Your options.* Think about your goals and how you can achieve them to find the perfect balance in both your professional and personal life. Assess whether the benefits of continued full-time employment are worth the associated pressures involved.

Remember: Life is not a dress rehearsal; it's the main event!

CHAPTER 2

Understanding and Dealing with Change

Pick a company, any company. It's a safe bet that in the near future, the organization will undertake or undergo some form of significant change. A division sell-off, a merger, a restructuring: the options are virtually unlimited, and new alternatives emerge regularly. Only one thing seems certain about the future: things will not remain as they are. The pace of change is unrelenting.

The world is changing so radically and quickly, in fact, that many of us struggle to understand what it all means. A business world that was once familiar, rational, and predictable has become confusing, irrational, and illogical. If you are contemplating any type or degree of change in your own career today, clearly you'll need to make your plans in the context of the broad change swirling about you. And even if you intend or hope to continue in a direction that is similar to what you've been doing for years, you'll still need to be aware of change.

> *The chances of any company being split within the next ten years are better than the chances of it remaining the same.*[*]
>
> Peter Drucker,
> American management
> consultant, author

[*]From *Managing in a Time of Great Change* by Peter Drucker. Reprinted by permission of Butterworth-Heinemann.

I have worked with organizations undergoing change for more than thirty years, advising management on business issues that affect people and profitability. In times of crisis, effective corporate recovery strategies need to be developed and implemented. In more stable periods, companies seek to anticipate change by restructuring operations. Whatever the situation, I've learned that change inevitably causes a dramatic and irreversible shift in the way work is conducted and perceived. There can be no doubt, as a result, that the world of work has also changed forever.

A SHORT HISTORY OF CHANGE

Workplace change is nothing new, of course. If we look through history, we find that different conditions called for different styles of work:

Historical Period	Work Style
Hunting and gathering age (tribal, village)	Flexible, needs driven, personal survival
Agrarian age (feudal, pastoral)	Flexible, seasonal, artisans
Industrial age (modern technology)	Time clock driven, inflexible, deskilled, process workers, functional specialization
Infotronics age	Time unfixed, flexible, creative, innovative, rapid change

What is different today is the pace of change. When many of us entered the workforce, we joined organizations that shared a common and simple career policy: "Leave it to us." If we did our job and remained loyal to our employer, we could expect our company to look after us.

Transfers and promotions at two-year intervals were the norm. Remain in the same position for much longer, and the signals were clear: you had stopped climbing the corporate ladder and were no longer on the path to career success. It may have had nothing to do with your performance. You might have upset your boss, or your boss's boss, or his secretary (your boss tended to be a "he" of course), or you might simply have been considered somewhat of a plodder.

Nothing endures but change.

Heraclitus (535–475 B.C.), Greek philosopher

During the 1980s, this policy was replaced with a more sinister term: "Offer and acceptance." The organization offered a position, and you accepted. The emphasis was on your accepting. All other choices tended to be career limiting.

A big bang occurred in the early 1990s when companies realized that because the quickening pace of change made it impossible to predict the future, they could no longer guarantee lifetime employment and job security. It was time for careers to become the responsibility of employees. Often, however, organizations didn't prepare their employees for this brave new world, expecting workers who had relied on employers for career development for decades to embrace the new reality with no preparation or training. Confusion reigned.

Some companies decided they could do their duty by producing self-help career development books. Others advertised jobs internally in ways that called for no previous training or experience—the career equivalent of offering people airplanes without asking if they had taken flying lessons. Not only did this cause people to feel confused and disoriented, but it also caused companies to experience significant losses in productivity and profit. It comes as no surprise that negative stress levels shot up, and organizational performance deflated.

No one is immune to change. In virtually all industries and countries, even CEO turnover is rising, as leadership changes are occurring more frequently than ever before. DBM (2000) recently conducted a global study of

> *We have to demand that people think through what constitutes the greatest contribution that they can make to the company in the next 18 months or two years. They then have to make sure that contribution is accepted and understood by the people they work for.*[*]
>
> Peter Drucker, American management consultant, author

CEO turnover and job security and found that nearly half of all CEOs have held their job for less than three years. In the past five years alone, close to two-thirds of all 476 companies in the study in twenty-five countries had installed a new CEO. The impact of this high turnover is directly shaping today's definition of corporate leadership: CEOs cannot help but adopt a short-term, high-payoff mind-set when it comes to planning and pursuing desired business goals.

We need to reflect on what is happening in companies to position ourselves for the greatest opportunity of personal and career satisfaction in the rapidly changing world of work.

[*]From *Managing in a Time of Great Change* by Peter Drucker. Reprinted by permission of Butterworth-Heinemann.

THE CHANGING WORLD OF WORK

Old World of Work	Today's World of Work
• Have job	• Do work
• Office	• Virtual space
• Success = Career ladder	• Success = Values, goals, and competencies aligned (career lattice)
• Authority	• Influence
• Status = Position	• Status = Impact
• Entitlement	• Marketability
• Loyalty to company	• Commitment to work and self
• Salaries and benefits	• Contracts and fees

- Job security
- Identity defined by job and organization
- Bosses and managers
- Employees

- Personal freedom and control
- Identity defined by life circumstances and work performed
- Customers and clients
- Vendors, intrapreneurs

Many of these new values are self-evident. Several deserve comment:

• *Have Job* → *Do Work.* In the past, we talked about "having a job." Today, even when a company formally employs us, we are far more likely to think of ourselves as independent vendors. We make choices about whom we will work for and what working environments we will consider working in.

"Having a job" is a passive pursuit. "Doing work" is an active process. The difference is fundamental and revealing. In fact, when we look at the differences underlying all these shifts from old to new paradigms, we find a single constant theme: we are responsible for our own careers.

• *Office* → *Virtual Space.* Traditionally, we have gone to an office, factory, or shop to pursue work. Technology is changing all that. Internet access, intranets, and videoconferencing now allow many of us to work from home, from the side of a swimming pool at a vacation spot, from a client facility, from an airport lounge (but not, please, from a cellular phone in a restaurant if I happen to be at the next table)—from almost wherever we choose. The result is that we have much greater freedom to blend work life and personal life than was ever possible in the past.

Most labor growth through to 2008 will be those aged 45+ years. This segment of the work force will increase from 33 percent to 44 percent. Those aged twenty-five to forty-four will drop from 51 percent to 41 percent. By 2012 more people will be leaving the workforce than entering.

DBM Research Study,
September 2001

Obviously, this doesn't apply universally. It is difficult to imagine managing a retail store from a distance, or maintaining a factory production line, or providing support services that require regular access to an office. But more and more options are now becoming available to more and more people.

The traditional distinction between leisure and work is becoming increasingly blurred. If 70 to 80 percent of the work that people perform in a modern organization is done by way of their intellects, is not work a process that goes on continually? People do not stop thinking just because they leave the office. Many people even work while sleeping. Ideas are processed in our dreams. This development also makes the classical distinction between home and office less relevant. In the blurred society, work is no longer a place. . . . it is an activity.

Jonas Ridderstråle and Kjell Nordström, Funky Business (2000).

• *Success = Career Ladder → Success = Career Lattice.* Many baby boomers have felt pressure—from family, peers, or even from society in general—to secure a steady job, work hard at it, remain committed to the company, and aspire to move as high up the corporate ladder as possible. In this life view, status has been seen as particularly important, and pride has been derived from achieving a senior level within a corporation. But the concept of aspiring to be a success within a company due to perceived external pressure is now dissolving, and that, I am convinced, is a wonderfully healthy trend.

A newer definition of success revolves around our own ability to accomplish whatever we choose. In this view, we move on a career lattice rather than a career ladder, which gives us far more flexibility throughout our careers, allowing us to gain skills across a wide range of competencies rather than simply focusing on a career ladder bounded by one narrow stream of activity. Approaching work from the perspective of the career lattice opens doors to more sustainable employability by increasing our career options and improving our ability to consider and succeed at a wider range of jobs and responsibilities. What we accomplish, not where we sit in the pecking order, is what determines success.

Rewired, Rehired, or Retired?

Ultimately, in fact, the greater latitude embraced by the career lattice can help us align our personal values and goals with our professional objectives, reinforcing and underscoring the value of achieving a balance between what is important to us at work and what is important to us in our personal lives.

• *Authority → Influence.* The old definition of work indicated that a job brought with it levels of authority that allowed one person to give instructions that other people were required to obey. In this view, a job title indicated a relative position of power and influence within an organization. Except in the most unusual circumstances, that authority was never to be questioned.

The new way of work is characterized by influencing through action. Here leadership becomes a function of skills, demonstrated achievements, clear competencies, and the ability to communicate the reason behind a decision or instruction. This ability to influence by our actions can lead to greater work satisfaction and greater achievements, both for ourselves and for the people who work with and for us.

• *Loyalty to Company → Commitment to Work and Self.* Loyalty has traditionally been an important corporate commodity. In the past, it was considered a two-way street: employees were loyal to the company, and the company rewarded them with job security and, up to a point, steady career progression followed by a gentle slide into retirement.

That was a well-meaning and honorable intention on the part of companies around the world. But on one continent after another, there came a time when economic and competitive realities made it impossible for employers to continue to provide such security to their employees. These same employers began to understand that in a newly competitive global workplace, their own continuing existence would be in question.

At first, and not at all surprisingly, many employees interpreted the shift as a betrayal: "I worked hard for them all these years, and look what they've done to me." More recently, people have come to understand that we are not being deceived by our employers; this is simply the way of work in a changing world.

In response to change, we need to make a new commitment to ourselves concerning our work. We need to look at ourselves as contractors working for a company of our choice, ensuring that our skills and experience remain current and questioning whether, given our needs and interests, we are in the ideal place.

One of the realities of this new and healthy contract between a company and its employees is that the employer openly admits (and we accept the premise) that it cannot guarantee job security. As an alternative, companies can agree to develop their staff and provide training and skill enhancement so that when and if individuals can no longer be employed by the organization, they can be assured of employability when seeking a job elsewhere. This is an important and valuable contribution. It means that employees, while committing themselves to the success of the company, can also think as free agents, keeping in mind that circumstances beyond anyone's control may mean they are looking for a new job tomorrow. And at the same time, just as the company is not betraying them if conditions force their departure at some point in the future, they are not betraying the company if opportunities come their way to pursue their careers elsewhere.

> The boss is dead. No longer can we believe in a leader who claims to know more about everything and who is always right. Management by numbers is history. Management by fear won't work. If management is people, management must become humanagement. . . .
>
> The job is dead. No longer can we believe in having a piece of paper saying job description at the top. The new realities call for far greater flexibility.
>
> Throughout most of the 20th century managers averaged one job and one career. Now we are talking about two careers and seven jobs. The days of the serving corporate man, safe and sound in the dusty recesses of the corporation are long gone. Soon, the emphasis will be on getting a life instead of a career, and work will be viewed as a series of gigs or projects.
>
> Jonas Ridderstråle and Kjell Nordström, *Funky Business* (2000).

In the end, one constant theme rings loud and clear: we are now responsible for our own lives. The world of work has changed forever.

At first we may find this difficult, particularly if we have grown used to a comfortable, cozy existence in which life is predictable and someone else makes decisions for us. This new world does demand adjustments, in that now we are responsible for making our own choices. But, realistically, who other than ourselves ought to be responsible for our futures? If we embrace the new realities, we are likely to find them exciting and rewarding, enabling us to do things we might never have thought possible and providing maximum opportunities for enjoying our lives to the full.

It is almost always worth taking a risk to move forward, even if the outcome is uncertain. Consider the times in your life when you've had to make serious choices that posed some level of risk: deciding to get married, buying a house, having a child, determining where your children will be educated. We have all been faced with such decisions in our lives, and for the most part, we've come through just fine. The changing world of work today shouldn't be any different.

> *If present demographic trends continue, the average worker in the 21st century will be aged over 40.*
>
> Margaret Patrickson,
> professor at the University
> of South Australia

REASONS FOR CHANGE

When Watson Wyatt (1995), the worldwide human resources consultancy, surveyed a thousand organizations in the United States that had made significant change through restructuring, the following statistics were revealed:

- Only 46 percent met their expense reduction goals.
- Fewer than 33 percent met their profit goals.
- Restructuring failed to produce the expected benefits 64 percent of the time.

This world of continuing change has caused a lot of pain for companies as well as employees. There are many reasons for change in our working environment and culture.

Restructuring and Retrenchment

According to a recent DBM survey (2000), performance typically has little to do with corporate retrenchments: over 70 percent of retrenchments were a result of restructurings, mergers, and acquisitions. Only a small percentage of affected employees lost their jobs for performance-related issues.

In a joint study conducted in Australia by DBM and the University of Southern Queensland (1996), employer-initiated moves such as restructuring and retrenchment rose from 14 percent over a ten-year period to 37 percent as the reason for recent job changes. Restructuring has emerged as an increased reason for job change, whereas promotion has been a decreasing reason.

Mergers and Acquisitions

In 1997, $1.6 trillion in merger deals were announced worldwide. By 1998, that figure had reached $2.5 trillion and in 2000, the figure rose yet again to $3.4 trillion (Thomson Financial Services, 2001).

One reason companies look to merge is to maintain the growth deemed necessary for survival. Mergers and acquisitions offer a quick way to attain the critical mass necessary for penetrating global markets, with the result that companies that once relied on organic growth for expansion can no longer afford the time and expense associated with that traditional growth strategy. Other reasons for mergers and acquisitions include gaining a competitive advantage, broadening the corporate asset base, developing new product capabilities, strengthening management and functional expertise, and increasing in size to reduce infrastructure costs and gain economies of scale.

Technology

The information age has not only eliminated jobs but has also changed how businesspeople communicate and manage. New technology enables small companies to compete globally while it eliminates the need for organizations to retain layers of managers to collect and dispense information. This availability of anytime-anywhere information has enabled developing countries, small companies, and enterprising individuals to attract capital to buy or develop technology and learn best business practices inexpensively. The Internet has demolished the traditional sales and distribution formulas for everything from cars to computers.

Globalization

Today, what happens in Asia, North America, Europe, or Latin America has a direct and immediate impact on customers and prospects around the world. As a result, there is increasing competition not only domestically but also globally.

Diversity

As the workforce becomes increasingly global, it is also becoming more diverse. Jobs no longer need to be filled from a local pool; anyone with talent, from anywhere in the world, may be considered.

Organizational Structure Redesign

Flattening an organization drives costs down, improves customer response time, and fosters strategic agility. Management guru Peter Drucker (1995) estimates that in the past ten years, most large companies have cut the number of layers of management by up to 50 percent. Employees who cannot or will not adapt to these new realities are likely to be among the first to depart.

Outsourcing

Companies around the world today are more likely than ever before to focus resources and management attention on a narrowly defined assortment of core competencies and priorities. Any function or activity—and the people responsible for it—that is not considered a strategic necessity becomes a likely candidate for outsourcing. As a result, there are now more temporary workers in the workforce than ever before. For example, 53 percent of the top one hundred businesses in Australia have outsourced major activities in the past twelve months (Howarth, 2001). Throughout the world, in fact, highly skilled workers, both technical and managerial, are now part of what has come to be called the contingent workforce.

Customer Focus

As customers worldwide demand and expect to receive what they want, when they want it, at a price they deem acceptable, a greater commitment to customer service has become a competitive requirement for most organizations. Companies not up to the challenge are being eliminated from the marketplace.

Consolidation

Increased consolidation in one industry after another has resulted in widespread organizational change. In Singapore, for example, the government has a policy to encourage local banks to merge with each other to consolidate the industry and create fewer but larger and stronger banks. This pattern is being followed all around the world, not only in finance but also in areas as diverse as petroleum, communications, and chemicals.

Given the range of forces at work in world markets today, it is abundantly clear that the world of work is vastly different than it was a decade ago. More to the point is the realization that the world of work ten years into the future is likely to be vastly different from today's workplace. We must adapt to change to survive and prosper.

People make capital dance.

Jonas Ridderstråle and
Kjell Nordström,
Funky Business (2000)

The one bit of good news in all this is that in businesses, people are the critical foundation. People are the true capital of any company.

DEALING WITH CHANGE

Given the scope and potential impact of change in the workplace, it is no wonder that most of us are wary of the phenomenon. In fact, in the wake of a significant change, we tend to feel a sense of loss and, whether we can articulate it or not, a need to reconcile or accept the fact that things will be different in the future. Our natural fear of change is grounded in the question,

Rewired, Rehired, or Retired?

"How is this going to affect me?" In this setting, it can be helpful to identify what has changed and what hasn't.

Different people manage the change journey or transition at different speed, intensity, and duration. What is important to recognize is that there is no "proper" reaction. In the face of change, anything—and everything—is normal. The experience can be felt as powerfully as the loss of a family member or the end of a marriage. As with these more personal events, unless there is grieving, people are likely to hang on to initial negative emotions and reactions and never adjust to the change. Unmanaged grief in a work environment creates problems with morale and productivity.

Understanding the process that people go through to adjust to change is the first step toward understanding the impact that change will have on the organization as well as the people who work there.

William Bridges, in his excellent book *Managing Transitions: Making the Most of Change* (1991)[*], highlights the complexity of change and stresses that change is not a single simple event: "In transition there is an ending, then a neutral zone, and only then a new beginning. But those phases are not separate stages with clear boundaries. The three phases of transition are more like curving, slanting strata in any situation. Or we might see them as overlapping." (See Figure 2.1.)

Figure 2.1. Three Phases of Individual Transition.

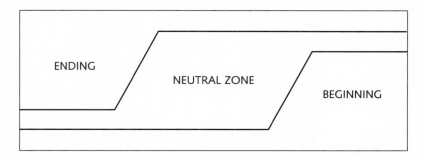

"In either case, you are in more than one of these phases at the same time, and the movement through transition is marked by a change in the *dominance* of one phase as it gives way to the next.

"It gets even more complicated. To give an example: in the changeover to a new information management system, you can be almost done (launching the beginning) at the same time you are just entering the transition caused by the recently announced reorganization (letting go of the old structure) and right in the neutral zone after last month's layoffs."

If your spirits are low, do something; if you have been doing something, do something different.

Author unknown

Bridges further writes: "We are constantly hearing about competitiveness, game plans, and winning. In a society as sports-minded as ours, those terms strike a ready chord—the more so when we seem to be falling behind in a game in which we were once the dominant player. But the sports metaphor is dangerously misleading. It suggests that there is a coherent game going on, and that the winners will come out ahead because they beat their opponents. It suggests that they win because they are a better team, with better talent, training, and strategy.

"In fact, a world of non-stop change offers only short-term victories to those organizations that set out to beat the opposition. The long-term advantage lies with those organizations that focus on the environment as a whole, not just on the competition. We are in one of those periods of evolutionary shift, and becoming preoccupied with the competition is shortsighted. It is not by competing but by capitalizing on change that today's organizations will survive. This is as true of a department or a project team as it is of organizations as a whole.

"The key to capitalizing on change lies in understanding and utilizing the cycle of challenge and response. As historian Arnold J. Toynbee demonstrated in his book, *A Study of History,* the great civilizations have risen to power not because of their advantages but because they

Rewired, Rehired, or Retired?

treated their disadvantages as challenges to which they discovered creative responses.

"Toynbee shows, for example, that Athens rose to dominance in the Classical world after its soil was depleted. Instead of being destroyed by that major setback, the Athenians treated it as a challenge to find a new way to participate actively in the economy of their day. Their creative response was to turn to the cultivation of olives, which could draw on much deeper water than could field crops. The Athenians rebuilt their economy around the export of olive oil, which further challenged them to build a merchant marine to transport it, a mining industry to create the coin to pay for goods, and a pottery industry to build the amphoras to contain the oil. New responses thus create new challenges at a lower level of the social organism.

You cannot create experience, you must undergo it.

Albert Camus (1913–1960),
French existentialist writer

"In a world undergoing non-stop change, every level of the organization must see its situation as a challenge, calling not for compliance but for creative response. When that happens, people are no longer victims who must wait and then act unquestioningly. Challenge and response restores a sense of control and purpose to people, no matter at what level of the organization they work."

ORGANIZATIONAL CHANGE

Businesses in the past have often viewed the older generation on their payroll as their obvious first choice to remove from their organization during tough times. Managers have focused more on cost cutting at the expense of losing their more experienced workers. At times, this has meant that a company has lost its history, which is not always the best solution for the long term.

During the mid 90s, when downsizing reached its peak, older workers were especially vulnerable. In the United States they were laid off at approximately five times the rate of their younger counterparts (Carnevale & Stone, 1995). During this period, the ratio of labor force non-participation rates to population for males aged 55 to 59 increased almost fourfold and for those aged 60 to 64 sevenfold. Male part-time workers in the same age groups doubled during this period.

Margaret Patrickson, professor at the University of South Australia

Given that major organizational change is inevitable in the face of current global trends, what is perhaps most important from our perspective is that it is the workforce that most often bears the negative impacts of change. But understanding that human resources represent a major corporate asset that should never be undervalued, businesses need to consider ways to manage employees and organizations alike. In fact, companies are coming to understand this reality. There is an increased awareness among organizations of the importance of aligning an individual's goals, values, and competencies with those of the organization.

Organizations need to develop and encourage a mind-set within their employees that enables them to be flexible and responsive to the developing needs of business and the market. This entails shifting the relationship between employer and employee from one of subordination to mutual benefit.

Companies best equipped to survive in this changing world recognize the different needs of individuals and the organization by developing frameworks, structures, and cultures that increase morale and productivity while reducing the traditional turnover and replacement costs associated with change. Organizations failing to recognize the need to help their staff cope with change generally do not reach their revenue and profitability goals and experience high levels of employee turnover.

With restructuring and retrenchment a fact of life, many organizations have proven they can do more with less, and they have invested significantly

Rewired, Rehired, or Retired?

in placing the right people in the right job roles and in managing and measuring the performance of employees.

You may have served a company well for twenty years and your historical track record is solid and partly relevant, but more important will be the future contribution you can make to a company that will ensure you are employable.

COMMON MISCONCEPTIONS ABOUT CHANGE

When people talk of the "good old days," often they seek a sense of permanence and continuity that they associate with earlier times. People hope that life might be the way they remember or imagine it to have been. There are a number of common misconceptions about change:

- Cradle-to-grave employment still exists.
- Good, hard-working people rise to the top and will be rewarded.
- Change happens quickly.
- Survivors of change are glad to have a job.
- Time heals all wounds.
- In the face of change, weak people leave the organization.
- If you're not "on board," there's something wrong with you.
- During change, people who seem to be okay really are okay.
- People hear what senior management communicates.
- If communication is done right the first time, communicating once is sufficient.
- It's possible to mandate a new organization.
- The behavior of senior management during a transition is invisible to the rest of the organization.
- Pressures that lead to change will be interpreted rationally.

> *Rules are made for people who aren't willing to make up their own.*
>
> Chuck Yeager (1923–), the first man to fly faster than the speed of sound

Corporations regularly fail to address these misconceptions, creating unnecessary stress for all involved, not to mention loss of productivity, profits and good people.

TAKE CONTROL AND EMBRACE CHANGE

Change has always existed in the world and will continue to be a constant in the future. There's nothing we can do to stop it, so we need to embrace change while working to maintain control of our careers and lives. We need to remain focused on our own values, competencies, and goals to maintain confidence and clarity of direction. Developing a mind-set that enables us to remain flexible and responsive to workplace change helps us face and deal with it more effectively.

> People who are 45+ today are the first generation to reach their late 40s with their numbers almost entirely intact.
>
> • They have been spared the ravages of disease.
> • Escaped participation in a major war.
> • Many are fitter and healthier than people of their age in previous generations.
> • Many are also looking forward to living longer than their parents.
>
> In the past people of this age may have been seen as "slowing down" and preparing for retirement. People in this age group today feel that they have got "a lot of living left to do."
>
> Mary Sparrow

DBM research (1999) has shown that in the years prior to the loss of a job, people tend to undertake fewer career-related activities: personal development, self-initiated performance appraisals, work-related reading, tertiary education, mentoring or coaching, active encouragement of feedback, or specific skill training, for example. People who retain their jobs in these situations typically are far more active and motivated in each of these areas.

Change not only creates the opportunity for fresh beginnings but also enables us to transform what we perceive to be a dangerous situation into something much better. That, in turn, helps us achieve a more enjoyable and fulfilling life. The challenge lies in working with change to create the work-life balance we aspire to.

It is only because of problems that we grow mentally and spiritually.

M. Scott Peck (1936–),
American psychiatrist and author

SUMMARY

The world of work has changed forever. We are now responsible for our own lives and careers and can no longer depend on a company for job security. Change inevitably causes a dramatic and irreversible shift in the way work is conducted and perceived.

• *A short history of change.* People fear change. To dispel the fear, it helps to identify what has changed over the years and what is now happening in companies to position ourselves for the greatest opportunity of personal and career satisfaction.

• *The changing world of work.* Now, in our competitive global workplace, the existence of job security is in question. We need to look at ourselves as contractors working for a company of our choice, ensuring that our skills and experience remain current and always questioning whether— given our needs and interests—we are in the ideal place. We are responsible for our future.

• *Reasons for change.* There are many reasons for change in our working environment and culture. These may include restructuring and retrenchment, mergers and acquisitions, technological advancements, globalization, diversity, organizational structure redesign, outsourcing, customer focus, and consolidation.

• *Dealing with change.* Given the range of forces at work in world markets today, it is abundantly clear that the world of work is vastly different than it was a decade ago. More to the point is the realization that the world of work ten years into the future is likely to be vastly different from today's workplace. We must adapt to change to survive and prosper. Different people manage the change journey or transition at different speed, intensity, and duration. What is important to recognize is that there is no "proper" reaction. In the face of change, anything—and everything—is normal. Understanding the process that people go through to adjust to change is the first step toward understanding the impact that change will have on the organization as well as the people who work for it.

• *Organizational change.* Organizations are rapidly embracing change to transform themselves into more efficient and effective operations. Organizations failing to recognize the need to help their employees cope with change generally do not reach their revenue and profitability goals and experience high levels of employee turnover.

• *Common misconceptions about change.* Misconceptions surrounding change blur the realities of change events. Many corporations fail to address these misconceptions, creating unnecessary stress for everyone, not to mention loss of productivity, profits, and good people.

• *Take control and embrace change.* Change has always existed in the world and will continue to be a constant in the future. There's nothing we can do to stop it, so we need to embrace change while working to maintain control of our careers and lives.

CHAPTER 3

Assessing Your Needs and Interests

If you enjoy what you do, you will never work another day in your life.
Confucius (551–479 B.C.), Chinese ethical teacher, philosopher

Have you ever known someone who said—and clearly meant it—"I can't believe I get paid to do this"? Such people have cracked the career code. Work is play for them. If you want to join those cheerful ranks, clearly you need to know what makes you fulfilled and contented.

STOP AND REALLY THINK ABOUT IT

When was the last time you took the time to sit down and really think about your career? I'm not talking about having a wayward idea interrupt your train of thought ("That was pretty dull") or pausing to make a casual observation ("I like this sort of assignment"). When have you cleared your desk and your mind and given serious consideration to a simple but potentially profound question: How does what I'm doing compare to what I would ideally like to be doing? To answer that question, you need to know just what it is that you'd ideally like to do.

Some of the most contented—and most successful—people I know make it a practice to reserve a full day each year to analyze what has gone on in the past twelve months, think about the things they enjoy in their careers, determine how well the two coincide, and, if they conclude that their needs and the facts of their work lives aren't synchronized, take steps to realign their needs and desires with the reality of their work.

But for a variety of reasons—time pressures come to mind, or perhaps the fear of discovering that we really won't like what we discover if we focus too closely on this—many of us are more likely to drift along, focusing on the task at hand, or this year's performance review, or next year's bonus. We assume that what we've done in the past is what's best for us. Why else would we be doing it day in and day out, after all?

As we move through life, our needs, priorities, and situations change, as do our skills, competencies, interests, and values. A career choice that might have been impossible to think about ten years ago, given the financial pressures of mortgages and college tuition perhaps, may be entirely practical today.

One thing is certain: if you don't ask yourself what would really make you happy in your work and your life and if you don't think about ways to reconcile the two, you will never know for certain that you've taken the best path, for both yourself and the people who are important in your life.

The good news is that the process of self-assessment doesn't need to be formal or painful to be profitable. Think of it as a kind of organized daydreaming, an exercise in no-strings-attached thinking about the best of all possible futures for you and the people you care about.

WORK SATISFIERS AND DISSATISFIERS

Begin the process by thinking about the things that satisfy and dissatisfy you in your work. After all, most careers contain things that make it enjoyable to head out to the job each day—things you can't wait to deal with. And at the same time, most careers also include responsibilities that, given the choice, you'd cheerfully do without. What things fall into each column for you?

Think about your current job and responsibilities. What do you particularly enjoy doing? What don't you like at all? Jot down a few notes for each category. Realize that there are no right answers to these sorts of questions. For every person who honestly loves the give and take and sharing of ideas and opinions that occur in a team meeting, there are others who would happily schedule a dentist's appointment to excuse themselves from the same meeting. For every individual who can't wait to start the research necessary to complete a written report, there is another who can't stand the process, putting it off until the last possible moment.

Don't just think about the tasks you complete in your work. Think about the organization and its culture too. What attracts you in your current work environment? What cultural elements could you do without?

Think back to other jobs you've held or other organizations you've worked for during your career. What tasks did you enjoy in those positions? What did you like and dislike about the culture at each organization? Are there certain things you miss in your current job that were present in the previous one?

Now try to identify patterns and draw conclusions from your thoughts. What themes emerge concerning the things you've enjoyed and not enjoyed as you've worked your way through your career? Try to summarize your conclusions in a list of personal satisfiers and dissatisfiers. Think in terms of both tangible (a steady paycheck, perhaps) and intangible factors (the opportunity to turn an idea into a product or service, say, or the chance to interact with a range of interesting people at work).

As you identify positives and negatives, consider their opposites. For example, if you find that having a great deal of freedom and latitude in your work is very satisfying, perhaps receiving detailed directions and regular reviews from a superior qualifies as a major dissatisfier for you.

Once you've created a list of satisfiers and dissatisfiers using the worksheet, rank both categories, putting the more important items at the top of your list.

Then sit back and think a bit about what all this might mean for your career. How well do your work satisfiers define your current position? How frequently do your dissatisfiers raise their ugly heads in your job? What might you do in response?

Satisfiers and Dissatisfiers.

What do you enjoy about your
current job and responsibilities?

What do you dislike about your
current job and responsibilities?

What attracts you to your
current work environment?

What irritates you about your
current work environment?

In previous job roles, what
tasks did you enjoy?

In previous job roles, what
tasks did you dislike?

Are you continuing to learn
in your job role?

Have you stopped learning
in your job role?

What other satisfiers can
you list?

What other dissatisfiers
can you list?

QUESTION YOURSELF

A variety of tactics will help you investigate career and life priorities. The questions that follow are designed to be thought prompters that will help you identify professional and personal goals as you work to gain a clearer sense of your future. As with the work satisfiers and dissatisfiers, obviously there are no right or wrong answers here either. Your only goal should be to be honest with yourself.

Answering questionnaires can be tedious, of course. Don't look at the lists that follows and think, "Uh-oh, this is going to take forever." Find a few areas that catch your attention, and think about them. Talk them over with your spouse or with a close and trusted friend. You might even ask that individual to answer some of them for you. What does he or she think makes you tick? Think of this as a process of discovery. And if you choose not to complete all the questions, that's fine too. It's up to you. But this type of guided introspection can help you challenge your own thinking about the future. By considering your answers to these questions carefully, your decisions for your future will become clearer.

> *The unexamined life is not worth living.*
>
> Socrates (469–399 B.C.),
> Greek philosopher

So take your time, answer as many questions as you can as honestly as possible, and you'll begin to visualize your future. Visualization is the first step to achieving your goals and achieving a work-life balance.

Achievements

- What are the highlights of your career to date?
- What have you achieved in your life, both professionally and personally?
- What have you done in the past twelve months that you are most proud of?

Current Responsibilities and Pressures

- Does your current career position increase your self-esteem?
- Do you crave more responsibility?

- What would you like to change about your current work situation?
- Do you respect your boss and colleagues?
- Are you proud to be involved with your company?
- Have you been recognized for your achievements?
- Do you feel under a lot of pressure to achieve unrealistic goals in the next six months?
- What makes you happy at work?
- What makes you unhappy or stressed at work? Have you taken any action to improve the situation? Is it impossible to reduce the stress?
- Do you have an aversion to new technology? If so, what are you doing to overcome it?
- Do you have career goals for the next six months? What are they?

Interaction with Others

- Are you a mentor to anyone?
- Do you maintain a network of career contacts?
- List twenty contacts, and note how each could help you in any way.
- How many of those contacts have you been in touch with in the past six months?
- List three people you would like to reestablish contact with, and state why.
- Do you enjoy team and other group activities?

Skills and Interests

- What are your top three interests?
- What new skills are you currently developing at work?
- Have you learned any new skills in the past six months?
- What new skills would you like to learn?
- What real or imaginary barriers are preventing you from developing these skills?

- Do you have a computer at home that you use on a regular basis?
- Do you need to improve your computer skills?
- Do you have strong communication skills?
- How can you improve your communication skills?

Options for Active Retirement

- Does the prospect of retirement appeal to you?
- Do you have any retirement plans in place?
- At what age do you intend to retire, and why?
- Are there employment areas you have identified to earn money during active retirement?
- What elements of retirement are you afraid of?
- If you did retire, how would you occupy your time?
- Do you have good time management skills?
- In the ideal world, would you like to work part time, full time, or not at all?
- Does temporary work appeal to you as a means of gaining more time for leisure activities?
- Are you prepared to adjust your lifestyle if your earnings are reduced?
- Are you financially set to maintain the lifestyle you wish?
- Can you get by financially without working?
- Do you have to work for money, or are you working because it's your lifestyle choice?

Family Relationships

- If you have a spouse or partner who is retired or works from home, how would he or she deal with your increased presence around the home if you retire?
- Have you discussed your plans with your partner?

- Do you share common goals with your partner?
- If you have children or grandchildren, do you spend enough time with them? If not, how can you make more time for them?
- What can you contribute to their development and well-being?

Support and Guidance

- Who can you turn to for guidance or advice?
- Which friends and family members are close enough to confide in?
- Who else can you ask for guidance or advice?
- Who do you consider to be your three closest friends?

New Challenges

- Do you want to start your own business, undertake contract or consulting work, or seek employment in a new field or with a new company?
- What sort of business would you like to operate?
- How much do you know about this industry?
- Are you prepared to risk your assets?
- Have you researched any self-employment opportunities?
- Do you enjoy new challenges in uncharted waters?

Fitness and Health

- Are you happy with your level of fitness?
- Are you happy with your appearance?
- If you could play any sport, which one would you most like to excel in?
- What form of exercise do you most enjoy?
- How often do you participate in this exercise?
- Do you have regular medical exams?

Rewired, Rehired, or Retired?

Hobbies and Travel

- What top three destinations in the world would you most like to visit?
- Why do they appeal to you?
- Are you able to make plans to go there in the near future?
- What is your favorite destination within four hours of your home?
- When was the last time you spent a weekend there?
- When do you plan to visit this destination next?
- What leisure activities give you the most pleasure?
- What is your favorite leisure activity goal?
- What are your most enjoyable social activities?
- Do you have any hobbies?
- Are there any new hobbies you would like to learn?
- Where are you going for your next vacation?
- When are you going to arrange it and make reservations?
- How often have you had to cancel a vacation in the past?

Personal and Career Goals

- Do you find personal fulfillment in your day-to-day activities?
- Are you willing to take risks to achieve your goals?
- List three things you have always wanted to do with your life, and explain why.
- What has prevented you from achieving these to date?
- What are your personal goals for the next three months?
- Who, if anyone, do you envisage doing these things with?
- What positively motivates you in the workplace?
- What positively motivates you in leisure pursuits?
- What plans do you have for future self-development?

- What other areas would you like to excel in?
- Can you achieve this by further study or communicating with key people?
- Does the idea of further study appeal to you?
- What would you like to study, and what would you benefit from it?
- What two career goals have you achieved in the past three years?
- How would you describe the week of your dreams?
- What's stopping you from achieving this?
- List three short-term goals (career, personal, or both)
- List three long-term goals (career, personal, or both)
- List three things you can do to improve your life immediately. Consider obstacles you may need to overcome.
- What is your action plan for the next year?
- What is your action plan for the next three years?
- Do you believe you can achieve a work-life balance that will give you personal harmony?

Consider your answers to these questions carefully. What are the main points that stand out? What makes you happy and gives you a sense of achievement and personal fulfillment in life? Most important, try to visualize actions you might take to make those things a greater part of your life.

Think in terms of a series of small steps, easily achieved wins that will give you a sense of growth and progress. Suppose, for example, that your self-assessment process reveals that you've always been interested in psychology but have never been able to find time to pursue the subject. Don't trip yourself up by thinking, "Well, I'd have to get a Ph.D., and I'll never have time or money for that, and I was never a great student, anyway." Think instead about someone you know and might talk to about your interest. Or spend a lunch hour finding a book about some aspect of psychology that particularly attracts you. Or search the Internet for readily available resources. Make it a game or a hobby, and see where that takes you.

Don't be surprised if your process of self-assessment uncovers broad new areas that interest you. Given the scope and pace of change discussed in Chapter Two, it's only natural that your needs and interests should have changed over time. Welcome the experience as a sign of growth and an opportunity for new development.

MAKE YOUR DREAMS A REALITY

Finally, never let yourself utter the self-defeating phrase, "I'm too old to . . ." You're not. You're fifty, give or take a few years, and there is no earthly reason that your best, happiest, and most rewarding years shouldn't lie ahead of you. Those years could be lived in a reenergized work environment, a satisfying retirement, or some combination of the two that fits your specific needs. Moreover, if you look back at what you've accomplished to date, you will probably find that you have gained the experience and possess the resources to fulfill your wishes.

> *Risk is what separates the good part of life from the tedium.*
>
> Jimmy Zero

SUMMARY

Taking the time to assess your current situation and whether it aligns with your work-life goals can make you aware of what needs to be achieved—or perhaps modified—to accomplish personal fulfillment.

• *Stop and really think about it.* When was the last time you took time to sit down and really think about your life and career? Take time out to think about your direction in life to discover if you've taken the best path for yourself and for the people who are important to your life.

• *Work satisfiers and dissatisfiers.* What do you particularly enjoy doing? What don't you like at all? Jot down a few notes for each category. What themes emerge concerning what you've enjoyed and not enjoyed as you've worked your way through your career? Try to summarize your conclusions in a list of personal satisfiers and dissatisfiers. Once you've created this list, rank both categories, putting the more important items at the top of your list. Then sit back and think a bit about what all this might mean for your career. How well do your work satisfiers define your current position? How frequently do your dissatisfiers raise their ugly heads in your job? What might you do in response?

• *Question yourself.* Consider your answers to the questions listed carefully so your decisions for the future will become clearer. What makes you happy and gives you a sense of achievement and personal fulfillment in life? Most important, try to visualize actions you might take to make those things a greater part of your life.

• *Make your dreams a reality.* If you look back on what you've accomplished to date, you will probably find that you have gained the experience and possess the resources to fulfil your wishes for a rewarding future.

CHAPTER 4

Understanding the Myths and Realities of the Mature Worker

As we begin to assimilate the material discussed so far, in terms of how work and life have changed in recent years and of what interests us within this environment, it begins to grow clear that conventional images of older workers probably haven't kept pace with reality.

Think about some of the things that have changed in our lifetimes:

- We were born before [color] TV, penicillin, polio shots, frozen food, copying machines, plastic and contact lenses.
- We were born before credit cards, split atoms, laser beams and ballpoint pens. Before tights, dishwashers, electric blankets, air conditioners, and drip dry clothes.
- We were born before house husbands, gay rights, computer dating, and computer marriages.
- We were born before day-care centers, group therapy and nursing homes.
- We had not heard of FM radio, tape decks, electronic typewriters, artificial hearts, word processors, pizzas, yogurt, instant coffee and guys wearing earrings.

- For us, time-sharing meant togetherness, not computers or holiday apartments in the Algarve.
- A chip meant a piece of wood. Hardware meant hardware and software wasn't a word.
- In our day, grass was mowed. Coke was a cold drink, pot was something you cooked in and rock music was a grandmother's lullaby.

No wonder we look different to those born around 1965; who came into a world of the Cold War, men walking on the Moon and the Pill.

And barely a decade later came the generation of DVD, DNA, personal computers, mobile phones, satellite television and the Internet.

Sidney Simkin – DBM UK

What do we really know, and what do we think we know about the career myths and realities confronting older workers today? In many parts of the world, there is a commonly held belief that older workers are likely to react differently to certain situations in the work environment than their younger colleagues. And—let's be clear about it—the implication lurking behind this view is that the older worker is going to be more rigid and less open-minded, that he will be risk averse and suspicious of change, or that she will look to the past, not to the future, for inspiration.

But how difficult, conceptually at least, is it to take that view and stand it on its head? What if we argue that by virtue of their ability to combine years of real-world experience with a lifelong sense of practical and intellectual curiosity, older workers actually bring more to the business table: a more valuable view of future opportunities grounded in hard-learned lessons from the past?

You don't need to look far for examples to support either point of view. During the dot-com craze of the late 1990s, for instance, people could (and probably did) tell you that anyone over the age of forty (or was it thirty, or even twenty?) could simply not be part of this phenomenon and, by implication, was excluded from the future of business. If you wanted proof, you

Rewired, Rehired, or Retired?

had only to look at stock valuations and the riches generated by initial public offerings. Youth rules.

Then, in 2000, when many of those stock prices imploded, people could (and probably did) tell you that on second thought, it probably would have made sense for those companies to have retained the experience of individuals who had actually developed a new product or created a new service at some point in their careers. Experience rules.

Now that the web's silly season is past, the grownups are taking over. During the internet gold rush, venture capital seemed to accept the 1960s mantra that nobody older than 30 could possibly be "relevant" to the new economy.

Now that the gold rush has ended—or at least headed to the islands for a rest—the target age for Silicon Valley execs has raced past 40. And 50-year-old CEOs are starting to look very attractive.

The end of the gale brings us into a phase I'm calling the "Revenge of the Old Guys." This is when executives who have been biding their time while their children ran amok are once again being handed the reins of power.

I can't cite hard numbers to prove this, but hiring qualifications are shifting toward experience, especially in tough markets, and away from raw ideas, youth and energy. What companies want today are people capable of leading them through difficult times.

So as dot-coms go belly up in the sudden death round, their youthful management teams are likely to get a rude awakening as to how their value is perceived.

Technology will continue to be an industry built on ideas and energy. And much of that will continue to come from super smart young people. But as we've learned, merely throwing venture dollars at kids isn't a sure path to success. And we should probably consider who's to blame—the venture capitalists throwing the money or the kids who caught it?

David Coursey, "Experience Counts: Revenge of the Old Guys,"
ZDNet News, November 8, 2000.

Everyone is unique, and career success, at any age, tends to be a function of the flexibility or inflexibility with which individuals respond to the work environment.

When I need to hire someone, an individual's education, training, and relevant experience are certainly important, but so are his or her enthusiasm, energy, and flexibility. It's the combination that makes a truly interesting candidate. Over the years, I have met thirty year olds who act like seventy year olds and fifty year olds with all the youthful vigor and optimism of twenty year olds.

It is important that we also recognize the necessary cultural fit, which can prove challenging when wide-ranging age groups work together. For example, a more mature person who has always worked in formal business attire may have difficulty adjusting his or her style if seeking employment at an information technology company with a team of predominantly young people who wear casual clothes. Also, some organizations create a closely knit culture, which may mean that some people who do not find such a culture appealing may have trouble adapting to it. This may be a function of that person's background and beliefs.

Why are flexibility and adaptability to change so important today? Because we live and work in an environment characterized by rampant, continuous change.

EVOLVING TECHNOLOGY

The constant spread of computers in our lives, the related introduction of new technology, and the new worlds of e-commerce and e-business can prove extremely frightening to people who are not themselves close to the development of technology. As a result, it is a common belief that older workers are averse to technology, and

In times of change the learners shall inherit the earth, while the learned find themselves beautifully equipped to deal with a world that no longer exists.

Eric Hoffer (1902–1983), American author and philosopher

especially to computer literacy. There are, of course, many exceptions, but the generalization still holds, and as long as it does, it can work to the disadvantage of mature workers.

Whether this is a reality or myth can vary by country and culture. Some countries are well advanced in computer technology, and workers in them have been forced to go with the flow. According to *Computer Economics* (1999), there will be 350 million on-line users worldwide by 2005.

Consider a simple example. If you are fifty years or older, you have undoubtedly experienced a revolution in business communications by witnessing—and being a part of—the following cycles of change:

> *To survive, to avert what we have termed future shock, the individual must become infinitely more adaptable and capable than ever before.*
>
> Alvin Toffler (1928–),
> American author

- 1960s: Relied on carbon paper to duplicate typing

- 1960s and 1970s: Made the move from manual to electric typewriters.

- 1970s and 1980s: Used telex machines

- 1980: Witnessed the widespread introduction of overnight courier services, fax machines, laser printers, and copiers

- 1990s: Saw the introduction and spread of e-mail dramatically change the speed, efficiency, and volume of communication

It is no secret that technology and technological change will never go away, and so whatever our age, we need to maintain acceptable levels of technological understanding and awareness. At a bare minimum, we need to be able to operate a computer with basic skills if we intend to be serious about having independence in our future careers.

Not having these skills isn't the problem. The key is for individuals to demonstrate that they are not averse to technology by enrolling in a program to gain relevant skills as quickly as possible. People who are embarrassed to admit their lack of technical savvy to their colleagues at work can enroll in a course outside work and buy a computer to start practicing at home, or they can hire their own computer-savvy child or teenage neighbor to help them.

COMMUNICATE EXPERIENCE EFFECTIVELY

As we mature, we confront a range of life experiences throughout our careers, building a great and precious reservoir of knowledge in the process. Our experience often creates feelings of déjà-vu, in fact, a sixth sense or premonition that helps us predict outcomes by comparing new experiences with similar situations from our past.

This experience is very valuable, as long as we continue to learn and unless we reach the point where we believe that we know it all. Many older workers who possess great skills and experience squander these resources by conveying information inadequately or inappropriately. Often, in fact, it is how knowledge is conveyed to fellow workers (and particularly to younger colleagues), rather than the actual knowledge itself, that has the greatest impact. If, for example, you have ever uttered a phrase similar to any of the following, you have probably caused younger colleagues to roll their eyes:

"I've been a manager for many years, so I know!"

"Don't question what I say. I have far more experience than you!"

"When I was your age, I showed respect for my superiors and appreciated their knowledge!"

Some older workers may need to rehearse and work through communication strategies. Developing this skill—and it is a skill that can be learned—allows the fact of life and business experience to shine through on its own. If we do not wish to contribute to the myth of older workers as yesterday's people peddling outdated knowledge, certainly we should never rely on our authority to try to get a message across.

Here is a suggestion: rehearse communication strategy and tactics with a younger friend or family member, and seek an open and honest reaction, which most people will gladly offer.

EXERCISING FLEXIBILITY

If you have worked for twenty or thirty years with one company or within one industry, you may be perceived as lacking flexibility. Ten to fifteen years ago, if you were applying for a job and could announce that you had worked for the same employer for a long time, that information would likely be taken as positive, because it demonstrated valuable traits of reliability, loyalty, and stability. Tell the same story today, however, and a potential employer may interpret longevity as a sign that you are risk averse, lack confidence, and are inflexible. The employer may look far more positively at a person who has assumed several roles in different organizations over many years. In the current employment climate, this is thought to reflect greater skills, broader experience, and more flexibility, all of which tend to be traits of valuable employees in today's career marketplace.

Do what you can, with what you have, where you are.

Theodore Roosevelt (1858–1919), twenty-sixth president of the United States

So how should you feel after reading the previous few paragraphs if you have worked for one company for twenty years? Obviously, you cannot change the facts of your career. But quite possibly your career has been a complete success within that one organization. And at the same time, you can balance the way your situation is perceived by identifying the many positives from your experience with the one organization.

Consider a banker who has worked for the same financial institution for twenty years or more. It is likely that this person has had exposure to numerous areas of expertise, has taken on many different roles, and has had to start new jobs in new locations with a new boss and new colleagues on many occasions. In the process, he or she has probably had wide-ranging experience in sales, accounting, customer service, human resources, strategic plan development, and management reporting. The fact that this person has worked with one company throughout these experiences does not have to hide the more important fact that in each new role and in every new location, he or she has done different jobs well while being evaluated closely by different superiors.

It is possible to break down the inflexibility myth by demonstrating a personal history of multiple careers within the umbrella of one organization.

OLDER WORKERS CAN'T GET JOBS (OR CAN THEY?)

One of the most persistent myths I hear from people around the world is that employers simply do not wish to hire people over the age of fifty or even forty. That, I am told, is the principal reason that older workers find it hard to secure new jobs. This may be due to several misperceptions:

- The older a person gets, the more that performance and mental ability decline.
- Older people are more expensive to employ than younger people.
- Older people are incapable of using modern technology.

In fact, however, a person who is not performing well at the age of sixty probably didn't perform well at the age of thirty-five either. In the absence of illness, intellectual ability rarely declines seriously before the age of seventy, and even that boundary is probably receding.

> People are much healthier in their fifties, sixties and even seventies than ever before, and there are more non-strenuous jobs from which to choose. In the Information Age, youthful strength is far less important than a worker's knowledge, dedication and experience—qualities that strengthen with maturity. The Commonwealth Fund, a New York based philanthropic group, recently sponsored research to determine whether worker performance declines with age. While productivity did fall off slightly when manual labor was involved, researchers found no correlation between age and work quality among supervisors and professionals.[*]
>
> Ken Dychtwald, *Age Power* (1999).

[*]From AGE POWER by Ken Dychtwald, copyright © 1999 by Ken Dychtwald, Ph.D. Used by permission of Jeremy P. Tarcher, a division of Penguin Putnam, Inc.

The world's largest organization of older people, the American Association of Retired Persons (1998), with more than 30 million members, surveyed employers' attitudes toward older workers. Older workers received ratings of "excellent" or "very good" on the following qualities (the percentages indicate the proportion of employers in the survey who gave these ratings):

- Attendance and punctuality, 86 percent
- Commitment to quality, 82 percent
- Loyalty to employer, 79 percent
- Practical knowledge, 79 percent
- Solid experience, 74 percent
- Reliable performance, 74 percent

My own experience has been that although it may be slightly more difficult and time-consuming for individuals over the age of fifty to find good new jobs, issues of perceived flexibility are far more likely to be involved than simple questions of chronological age.

Within the worldwide DBM business, we undertake statistical research annually on the people who have been in our outplacement programs to determine the average time they take to get back in the workforce. In recent years, we have also analyzed the average time people under age fifty and over that age have taken to get a new job.

The bad news is our research supports the view that older workers do need more time. The good news is that over the past three years to December 2001, people over the age of fifty on outplacement programs require approximately only four weeks longer to return to the workforce than people under age fifty. True, some older workers prefer to seek contract work, consulting assignments, or project assignments and not traditional career-type employment. But the conclusion is very clear: older workers who are well prepared and demonstrate energy, flexibility, and focus can normally get good jobs. Like anyone else, they have to make getting a job a full-time job, not a part-time occupation that they fit in between tennis games. But the opportunities are there to be seized. This research was consistent across many countries around the world in which DBM operates.

A good example of a company that has learned the value of employing older workers is the Vita Needle Company, based in Needham, Massachusetts. The sign on the factory door states "Help Wanted. Light machine operators. Part-time. Employees set own hours/days. Predominantly senior citizens. No retirement age."

Why does Vita Needle hire seniors? In the 1980s, the company was pressured to expand its line of medical products due to the spread of AIDS. Initially it began recruiting older workers because they were reliable and inexpensive. In addition, management appreciated that 65+ workers were very careful and tended to have half as many work-related accidents as younger workers. Management also came to regard them as harder-working, more loyal, and less prone to personal problems than many younger workers. Vita Needle's annual sales have grown by 20 percent every year for the past five years. Average age of Vita Needle employees: 73.

Similarly Travelers Insurance has taken a leadership role in using older workers by creating a job bank of temporary employees from a pool of retirees. The higher productivity of these workers has saved Travelers $1.5 million a year. General Electric has discovered that it is more economical to retrain veteran engineers in emerging technologies than to hire new ones. The Boeing Corporation regularly brings back capable retirees to help with new aircraft production. Likewise, Bonne Bell, the cosmetics manufacturer in Westlake, Ohio, created a "Seniors Only" production group—the brainchild of chairman and CEO Jess A. Bell, himself 74.

The trend toward rehirement, not retirement, will accelerate as more aging trendsetters such as Jimmy Carter, Warren Buffett, Lee Iacocca, Beverly Sills, Barbara Walters, John Glenn, Sean Connery and Helen Thomas make it "in" to remain productive in maturity.[*]

Ken Dychtwald, *Age Power* (1999).

[*]From AGE POWER by Ken Dychtwald, copyright © 1999 by Ken Dychtwald, Ph.D. Used by permission of Jeremy P. Tarcher, a division of Penguin Putnam, Inc.

Rewired, Rehired, or Retired?

THE VALUE OF OLDER WORKERS AND MENTORS IN SMALLER COMPANIES

The realization is now increasing among organizations that a more experienced worker may be more of an asset than a liability.

> A little seasoning can spice up your company culture. "Seasoned" executives have already learned the valuable business lessons that young start-up entrepreneurs have yet to acquire. Recruiters say fast-growing small businesses are clamoring for older workers. Search firms across the country have been inundated with requests for experienced marketing executives, CFOs and CEOs. "Grey Hairs" can bring leadership skills and increased visibility to a small firm struggling to make a name for itself. However, management-level candidates are becoming increasingly difficult to recruit. Experts say the best way to snag a corporate heavyweight is through grassroots networking practices: ask clients for referrals, post jobs in industry newsletters and on web sites and announce openings at trade conferences.

Older workers, in fact, have advantages in today's job market. One of the virtues of experienced employees who have worked for different companies or have undertaken many roles within one company is that they gain wide-ranging skills and knowledge in the process. They did not focus on one small part of a business—sales, manufacturing, accounting, or distribution, for example. Rather, they have been exposed to multiple areas of work throughout their careers.

Particularly in smaller companies, where, after all, a high proportion of new jobs are being created today, a more experienced worker can be extremely valuable. A company owner, who may be younger, can use this pool of valuable knowledge to help build the company, leveraging his or her own life experience with the potentially broader qualifications of older colleagues.

Ironically, however, because older workers gain so much experience and become highly skilled in so many areas, they sometimes assume that everyone has similar knowledge, downgrading their own perceived value to a company. It is important to reflect on individual strengths and experience and recognize that age represents a valuable asset to any organization.

Experience can add an entirely new dimension to a younger company. With the explosion of new industries and the development of e-commerce, and with many young entrepreneurs developing new businesses today, an older worker can play a valuable role of support as a mentor without being viewed as a threat to the job security of the people in the organization. With the right attitude, a seasoned performer can provide immense value as a mentor and prove to be indispensable within a young company.

If you didn't answer the questions in Chapter Three to assess your needs and interests, perhaps now is the time to revisit them.

TRANSFERRING SKILLS BETWEEN INDUSTRIES

Here is a quick career quiz: How are the dairy, banking, power distribution, and petroleum industries similar? The answer is that each industry sells a generic product, and success in each industry depends on how well it manages its raw materials. Milk is milk wherever it is sold, cash is cash, one unit of electricity is the same as the next unit of electricity, and the same applies to gasoline or diesel fuel, which can be supplied by many refineries.

Above all, challenge yourself. You may well surprise yourself at what strengths you have and what you can accomplish.

Cecile M. Springer,
American businesswoman

Companies in each industry rely on the skills of their employees to differentiate them from their competitors and ensure that an appropriate distribution network exists to move their products to consumers. Competitive success also requires sound marketing and good selling skills.

People who worry about declining employment opportunities in any of these industries or who lose or become dissatisfied with a job in one of them are not dissimilar from people who deal with the products sold and distributed in any of the others. In the banking industry, for example, mergers and acquisitions have eliminated numerous jobs in recent years. With continued consolidation in the financial sector, people who have been dislocated by this process cannot simply turn to another bank for a new job. But it is important to note that the vast majority of them were never involved in the creation of cash; instead, they dealt with the distribution of cash by packaging it, marketing it, and distributing it in various ways to different client segments.

Individuals investigating new employment horizons need to view themselves as a product and develop appropriate marketing strategies while recognizing that opportunities are occurring in other industries to which their skills can be transferred. In fact, as much as 95 percent of the skill and experience needed to succeed in a new cross-industry job is likely to be a function of a person's transferable skills. The remaining 5 percent consists of new industry knowledge. This knowledge can be learned, and often very quickly.

The most experienced workers have often already worked in more than one industry, bearing testament to the reality of the ability to transfer skills.

BE YOURSELF . . . ALL OF YOURSELF

Ethically, practically, and professionally, of course, we should never disguise our age or try to reinvent previous job positions or responsibilities. To the contrary, we have an opportunity to use our experience as a strength, demonstrating that we have wonderful skills that can be very adaptable across a wide range of industry sectors.

> Harland Sanders, born on September 9, 1890, was only six when his father died and at the age of ten he got his first job working as a farm hand earning $2 a month. He held a series of jobs over the next few years, first as a streetcar conductor and then, at sixteen, he lied about his age and joined the army as a private, soldiering for six months in Cuba.
>
> After that he was a railroad fireman, studied law by correspondence, practiced in justice of the peace courts, sold insurance, operated an Ohio River steamboat ferry, sold tires, and operated

service stations. When he was forty, Harland began cooking for hungry travelers who stopped at his service station in Corbin, KY.

As more people started coming just for food, he moved across the street to a motel and restaurant that seated 142 people. Over the next nine years he perfected his secret blend of eleven herbs and spices and the basic cooking technique that is still used today.

In the early 1950s a new interstate highway was planned to by-pass the town of Corbin. Seeing an end to his business, the Colonel auctioned off his operations. After paying his bills he was reduced to living on his $105 Social Security checks.

Confident of the quality of his fried chicken, the Colonel devoted himself to the chicken franchising business . . . and you know the rest of the story.

Until his death in 1980 at the age of ninety, the Colonel traveled 250,000 miles a year visiting the KFC empire he founded. And it all began with a sixty-five-year-old gentleman who used his $105 Social Security check to start a business.

KFC, *The Story of Colonel Harland Sanders* (2001).

SUMMARY

Everyone is unique, and career success at any age tends to be a function of the flexibility or inflexibility with which individuals respond to the work environment.

The key to converting old career myths into new employment realities is primarily a function of personal attitude, communication style, commitment to being aware of new technology, and, perhaps most important, personal and professional flexibility in a changing world of work. Get the attitude right, and the rest will follow.

I know a number of older people who are able to communicate and interact effectively with people of all ages, because they are excited by life and their interest and optimism are reflected in their whole being. They can engage the interest of a young person just as surely as they can someone of their own age. If you take a moment to reflect, I am sure you can think of similar people you know, and perhaps you can use them as role models to develop how you communicate with people of all ages in the workforce. Perhaps you are already a role model.

Remember the following key messages when it comes to separating the myths from realities relating to the older worker:

- *Evolving technology.* Whatever our age, we need to maintain acceptable levels of technological understanding and awareness. The key is to demonstrate that you are not averse to technology by enrolling in a program to gain relevant skills, if required.
- *Communicate experience effectively.* As we mature, we confront a range of life experiences throughout our careers, building a great, precious, and extremely valuable reservoir of knowledge in the process.
- *Exercising flexibility.* A potential employer may interpret longevity in a job as a sign that you are risk averse, lack confidence, and are inflexible. It is possible to break down the inflexibility myth by demonstrating a personal history of multiple jobs within the umbrella of one organization.
- *Older workers can't get jobs (or can they)?* Older workers who are well prepared and demonstrate energy, flexibility, and focus can normally get good jobs.
- *The value of older workers and mentors in smaller companies.* A more experienced worker can be extremely valuable to a company owner, who may be younger, who can use this pool of valuable knowledge to help build the company. Older workers can play a valuable role of support as a mentor without being viewed as a threat to the security of others in the organization.
- *Transferring skills between industries.* Individuals investigating new employment horizons need to view themselves as a product and develop appropriate marketing strategies while recognizing that opportunities are occurring in other industries to which their skills can be transferred.
- *Be yourself. . . all of yourself.* Never disguise your age or try to reinvent previous job positions or responsibilities. It is important to use your experience as a strength, demonstrating that you have wonderful skills that can be very adaptable across a wide range of industry sectors.

If you let it, in fact, age can prove to be an advantage rather than a disadvantage.

Self-Assessment: Flexibility and Adaptability.

Reflecting on this chapter, assess your flexibility, experiences, and ability to adapt to change by responding to the following questions:

Have you learned current technology to a level that you can work efficiently on your own?

Have you been able to use your experiences in a positive way to motivate others?

Are you prepared to listen openly to a point of view that is different from yours and objectively assess its merits?

Can you give examples where you have shown flexibility in a situation where the safer route would have been to stick to the rules?

Have you been in situations where you have been able to move the focus of a discussion away from your age and toward your ability?

Do you have younger people seeking your advice, or do they avoid you?

Have you been able to transfer your skills from one job or industry to another successfully?

Do you embrace or fear change?

Rewired, Rehired, or Retired?

CHAPTER 5

Achieving a Level Playing Field with Younger Workers

You can't teach an old dog new tricks.
or
It's never too late to learn.
                    Traditional sayings

Older workers are easy to typecast because the myths persevere:

• They're less effective on the job than younger people.

• They don't deal well with change.

• They look to the past, not the future.

• They examine and reexamine, taking forever to reach a decision.

• They want to be rewarded for loyalty, not performance.

It's so easy to typecast senior workers, in fact, that these views have contributed to the notion of the unemployability of seasoned people. In fact, if you substitute *experienced* for *older* and view the situation from that perspective, you can dismiss the stereotypes and turn the myths into strengths.

No matter what your age, if you can demonstrate flexibility, show the right attitude in a range of situations, remain open-minded, and keep yourself alert to new ideas and new ways of thinking, all the while putting your experiences to good use, you can dispel the myths. Simply being aware of the valuable assets you have developed and assembled throughout your career lets you position yourself to make valuable contributions when you work with, and even achieve an advantage when you compete against, younger workers.

This chapter primarily focuses on using your experience to achieve an advantage during the job search process. But virtually all of these suggestions and observations apply just as well to almost any other business situation.

You have certainly had many valuable experiences throughout your career. Think back to achievements for which you were complimented or perhaps even promoted. No doubt you can also recall events and situations that didn't work out quite so well. Don't ignore them! Realize that they too represent important learning experiences.

The key here is that because you have lived life and developed some level of business wisdom during your career, you can draw on your past to plan and take advantage of your future. There is no substitute for experience. It gives you a natural advantage over less experienced workers, but only if you use it wisely.

CAPITALIZE ON YOUR EXPERIENCE

The human brain, a three-pound mass of interwoven nerve cells that controls our activity, has an amazing capacity to store information. Still, estimates suggest that we use only about 10 percent of our brain's capacity. The more we learn, the more the brain can retain for future reference.

The simple fact that you've been working for more years gives you a potential advantage over younger workers. Think of the times you've come up with a solution to a problem by drawing on a recollection of an experience that has occurred in your past, perhaps even a decade or more ago.

Lessons from Experience.

On this page, list your valuable experiences and what you have learned from them. Experiences can be taken from any or all of the following categories:

- Success stories

- Experiences where things didn't work well or go as planned

- Experiences in your family or social environment

- Experiences in your current or previous job

- Experiences gained while growing up

And do not think that you can learn only from successful experiences. You've also learned from your mistakes and the mistakes of others. In retrospect, the lessons that offer the greatest wisdom come from the experiences that didn't work out as well as we'd hoped or planned.

One of my most indelible career experiences came from my days in banking, when I recommended a loan for a customer for the development of a hotel. The development did not proceed as well as planned, and the customer could not repay the loan. I lost a great deal of sleep over the situation, treating the situation as if it was my own money at risk. Eventually, I resolved the problems, thanks to significant research, meetings, and negotiations, with the result that the asset was sold to another company, at no loss to my bank. It was also good news for the customer, as we were able to work closely with this person in a supportive manner and stave off financial ruin.

The lessons I learned during those months never left me. The experience made me a better banker. From then on, I was careful to take all necessary precautions to prevent the same situation from happening again. Over time, that resulted in much higher profits for my employers. I still apply the same caution in any business dealing today. It doesn't mean I still don't make mistakes. It's just that the mistakes are smaller than they otherwise might have been.

When I went to university as an older student after I was married to complete my economics degree, I was bombarded with information. I wondered how I could ever apply so much information in real life. I remember one of my lecturers telling me it was highly likely I would only use 5 percent of what I was learning in the business world. This was extremely discouraging. Was 95 percent of what I was learning really going to be wasted?

Following college graduation, my career exposed me to a wide range of banking in different countries around the world. Although a great deal of what I had learned in college was not relevant right away, I now look back and realize I have been able to draw on the majority of that knowledge, applying it at key points in my working life.

RESEARCH AND REHEARSE

As you rely on your experience, take care to think before you leap: consider the situations and conditions that confront you before taking action. Suppose, for example, that you have reached the career decision to seek work with a new company. Before approaching the organization, you would be wise to conduct some research to determine its style and culture and then adapt your experience to what you have learned.

With the Internet, the ability to research a company sits at your fingertips. You can obtain an enormous amount of on-line information about most large companies: industry information, competitor data, and economic forecasts, for example, as well as details of corporate structure and the identities of key decision makers. There is no excuse for going to an interview without having a good working knowledge of a company and its operations.

Recently, a colleague and I were astounded when we conducted interviews with a final panel of job applicants presented to us by a search firm for a very senior role in our company. We started to ask specific questions about how each candidate could add value to the company. My associate and I almost fell off our chairs when the first candidate's responses made it clear that he thought we were a search and recruitment firm. Either he could not understand, or did not care enough to learn, the significant differences between outplacement and recruitment. (Need I say we chose someone else for the job?)

Asking the right questions takes as much skill as giving the right answers.

Robert Half,
American businessman

Researching a company thoroughly prior to an interview or in advance of any other business contact prepares you for questions that may be asked, identifies areas you may wish to learn more about, and, most important, gives you added confidence that you have put in the necessary preparation to present yourself effectively.

If the meeting is a job interview, rehearse the key questions you are going to ask, along with your answers to inquiries you anticipate, and even practice them with colleagues or friends who know the recruiting firm or employer you will be talking to. Seek their feedback to make sure that your communication style meshes with that environment. If you have a friend or acquaintance in the recruiting industry, so much the better, even if that person's expertise is in a different industry segment. Ask the person for honest feedback on your style and interview skills.

IDENTIFY DIFFERENTIATORS

To establish yourself as the most suitable choice in a job search campaign, take the time to develop a list of differentiators to make you stand out from the crowd. Differentiators come from the depth of experience you have gained in your career. And remember, by virtue of your years of business experience, all other things being equal, you should have more and better differentiators than younger applicants do.

You might demonstrate an advantage in a number of ways:

- Ask questions that show that you are sensitive to the interrelationship of various parts of the business.

- Prove you have the ability to research an industry and understand its potential future.

- Show respect for a potential colleague or superior by showing empathy regarding the challenges the company and he or she may be facing.

- Illustrate your experience with examples showing how you might give value-added to the company for the specific job. Don't be afraid to share some ideas that may help the company.

- Communicate sensitively that you have additional skills to offer that may be extremely valuable—for example, for special projects or feasibility studies.

- Inquire about and understand the mission statement or business plan of the company to show how your strengths and aspirations align with the goals of the company.

COMMUNICATE POSITIVELY

Having the right attitude goes a long way in job search and career advancement. Why shouldn't you be the best-suited candidate for the position?

If you find yourself out of work, it is natural to feel concerned, or even desperate, about finding new employment. Such feelings tend to be reflected in body language and style of communication, and that can be off-putting to an interviewer. If you are aggressive, agitated, or critical of others, you do nothing to help your cause. Interviewers easily pick up on negativity, so keep this in mind.

In the same vein, never criticize a former employer in a meeting. If you have had a bad experience, it may be hard to block the event out of your mind, but if you continue to focus on the past, you cannot start living for tomorrow. It's important to accept the reality that the past cannot be changed. Start to think in terms of all the wonderful opportunities in the world that can make tomorrow exciting. Once you begin to think this way, you will start to feel more positive, and this will be reflected not only in an interview but also in your whole attitude to everyone you encounter.

Reflect back on the companies that you have worked for or the positions you have held. It is extremely valuable to believe that you work for the best company with the best people, products, and services. When you believe this, it becomes natural and easy to support and promote the company's services and products.

Now apply this same logic to yourself. Do you believe you are the best candidate for a job role? If you don't, how can you expect to be successful and win the job?

Examining your skills and experience, your attitudes and enthusiasm will help remind you that you are the best candidate for the job. If you can

Think about the successful people you know. Chances are they feel good about themselves. Optimism takes practice. The great thing about cultivating a positive outlook is that you can practice all day long without taking any extra time out of your schedule.[*]

Patricia Mansfield, author

do that, it is amazing how often you will be successful. It's like a sprinter who visualizes running a perfect race and then goes out and sets a personal record. Why should you be any different?

It is always important to be sensitive to, and with, your audience, whether it's a single interviewer or a group of potential colleagues. You may even want to fine-tune your presentation style to reflect the interview environment, as long as you do not lose any of your own personality or individuality in the process.

Here are some tips to ensure positive, sensitive communication:

- Don't respond negatively to questions. Position your answers in a positive manner by referring to difficult situations as challenges, opportunities, or even learning experiences.

- Don't criticize a previous employer or competitor. Highlight the positive aspects of what you've achieved wherever you've been.

- Don't dwell on situations where you have been harshly treated in the past. (The interviewer is unlikely to be interested).

- Avoid highlighting the fact that you have previously been in positions of authority and therefore know how to do the role of the person interviewing you. If you are passionate about the opportunity, your knowledge will naturally shine through.

- Don't try to speed things up for future discussions. Asking about the next steps in the process is a legitimate question, however.

[*]Reprinted from *Why Am I Afraid to Be Assertive* by Patricia Mansfield. Published by HarperCollins Publishers Ltd.

- Don't present yourself aggressively. Smile and present in a careful and logical way.

- Be aware of your speech. People who are nervous often speak too fast and even forget to breathe regularly.

- Be aware of your body language. Avoid slouching, folding your arms, or tapping your fingers.

- Maintain eye contact with people who are speaking to you.

- Determine the personality style of the interviewer, and adapt your communication style to suit that person. (We delve into this topic in more detail in Chapter Six.) Look for signs that will help you—for example:

  If someone has family photographs in his or her office, consider sharing some information about your family. It will be a common bond and will provide the interviewer with further information about the type of person you are.

  If an interviewer's office is filled with charts and business figures, position your questions and responses in a no-nonsense way.

  If the interviewer has trophies or photographs with dignitaries, ask about them.

- Remember that one goal in an interview is to make the interviewer feel comfortable with you.

- Nerves can hinder your memory. Maintain concentration throughout the interview.

ALIGN WITH YOUR GOALS

Throughout the job search, always focus on the type of work-life balance that is best for you. When you apply for a job, make sure it fits with your work-life vision and you feel comfortable about the culture.

Younger workers often take jobs without thinking about the consequences of their decisions in terms of career direction, cultural fit, and alignment of goals and values. A more mature worker has more at stake. You have already had years of experience, climbed career ladders, and achieved many goals. Make sure that the next step is aligned with your current goals.

In an interview, don't be afraid to share your thoughts about the desire to have a work-life balance. It is far better to learn in an interview that a work environment may not be right for you than to come to that realization after you've been appointed to a position. If you believe the environment is not right for you, be honest. Be prepared to share your reservations in a constructive manner, or simply thank the interviewer and suggest that you leave.

The message you want to convey is that if you are successful, you want to be a valuable employee, and you want the decision to be right for you and the company. This approach, which takes courage, can increase your chances for success. Companies are looking for talented people who are prepared to think and want to make a contribution. Most interviewers will respect the fact you are concerned with ensuring you can align with the company's goals and its values. This will assist in positioning yourself over younger workers.

LISTEN CAREFULLY

One of the rarest business skills is the ability to be a good listener. So often, in their exuberance to demonstrate their skills and experience, people spend far too much time talking and not nearly enough time listening.

You can gain an advantage over younger workers by listening carefully to what people say in an interview, absorbing what you've heard, offering intelligent feedback, and indicating your interest and professionalism by the quality of your questioning.

As a more mature worker, you should have the ability to respond to questions well while also demonstrating clear listening skills. If you are a good listener, you will collect valuable clues that will help you with your questions and answers to achieve greater success. (See Chapter Six for more tips on being a good listener.)

We have one mouth and two ears. We should use them in that proportion!

TAKE CARE WITH YOUR PERSONAL PRESENTATION

Taking pride in yourself by showing good hygiene and good grooming, as well as maintaining your physical health, goes a long way in any business situation. The importance of good personal presentation makes it necessary to be aware of your appearance to remove some of the possible negatives that may be associated with older workers.

Personal grooming has a significant effect on how others respond to us. Clean clothes, hair, fingernails, and shoes go a long way. If an interviewer notices that you're wearing dirty, tired-looking shoes, this may be interpreted to reflect a lack of attention to detail or even a lack of self-image on your part.

Look at your wardrobe. When was the last time you bought new clothes? Staying current with every fashion trend isn't the objective here, but keeping abreast of what is currently fashionable is important. For example, the width of ties, suit styles, clothing fabrics, and skirt and dress lengths change over time. Moreover, the growing acceptance of business casual dress has fundamentally changed the definition of dressing for business success. You may have to dress in a business suit for an interview at an investment bank and more casual wear for an interview at an Internet company. You certainly do not want to show up in khaki pants and a sport shirt, only to be met by an interviewer wearing a three-piece suit. Or if you wear a suit to a company where everyone dresses casually, your ability to fit in with the company style and culture may be questioned. As a result, effective personal presentation for an interview requires a little research. Find out the style of the company and the most suitable style of dress for the interview. Whatever the environment may be, be careful not

> *He who has health has hope. And he who has hope has everything.*
>
> Arabian proverb

to lose your own identity in trying to conform.

If you've been wearing the same old clothes for the past ten years, it is amazing how differently you will be received if you have a fresher look. If you admire the clothing style of a friend or colleague, consider asking him or her for help. Particularly because your self-esteem may suffer a bit during a period of job search, updating your look (if your finances permit) may help lift your self-confidence. Consider not only clothes but shoes, glasses, and even a new hairstyle. Do not, however, try to dress like a twenty year old (unless you are a twenty year old). It doesn't work, no matter what shape you're in. It's best to stick to a dress style that you feel comfortable with; otherwise, you could feel silly and even look a little ridiculous.

DEAL EFFECTIVELY WITH SEARCH AND RECRUITMENT FIRMS

Many companies seek the assistance of recruiting firms to identify suitable personnel for open positions. But although there are many experienced professionals in this industry, there are also others who are more focused on gaining a placement fee than caring about, or taking care with, the individuals they interview for the position.

Case Study: Persistence Pays

In Peru recently, a sixty-five-year-old man became a participant in the DBM program when his position was eliminated following a merger at the brewery company at which he worked. He had been a logistics manager, expert in empty bottle handling (most breweries in Peru use returnable bottles).

Not long after arriving at DBM, he spotted a newspaper advertisement seeking someone with his expertise. He sent his resumé. Nothing happened.

Three weeks later, the same advertisement appeared. He sent his resumé once again. Again nothing happened.

Two weeks later, the same advertisement appeared again, and he sent his resumé a third time. This time, he was contacted a couple of days later by the brewery that had advertised the position. He was ultimately hired as its logistics manager.

Later, when he asked why he had not been contacted after his initial approaches, the plant manager said he had twice hired people based on the recommendation of the search firm he was using and had twice fired the hired people because they were good in logistics but had to learn the secrets of empty beer bottle handling. The third time he advertised the position, he requested to see every incoming resumé. While reviewing them, he saw the DBM candidate's resumé and called him immediately. The reason the search firm had not considered our candidate was that they thought he was too old.

The problem you may face in a recruiting firm interview is that in many cases, recruiters stick closely to the job specification and as a result may not want to be seen to be suggesting a mature worker for a position if the specification does not expressly call for one. Age discrimination is not permitted in theory, of course, but a lack of flexibility can surface when it comes to formal job specifications. Some recruiting professionals have the confidence and work experience to challenge their clients by suggesting variations from the job description given to them.

This presents a real challenge, because you will not be talking to a potential employer, who may see your skills and experience and recognize the value you could bring to the company, even though your skills, age, and experience are not precisely aligned with the initial job description.

Still, although it is important to be aware of the negatives in dealing with the recruitment industry, remember that many recruiters have the experience, confidence, and awareness to look beyond the job specification. They can combine their knowledge of a company and its culture in a much more positive way to identify your suitability for an organization.

If you know someone who works for the company that has retained a search firm, you might ask that person to introduce you to the employer directly. This is likely to be an exception more often than a rule, but it does offer a strategy for overcoming the prejudice of a recruiter. Most important, if you take this route, communicate with the recruitment firm following your meeting so that you will be seen as open and honest at all times.

In my career, I have received such requests on several occasions. If I respect the person contacting me and know that he or she is not just doing someone a favor but legitimately believes I should consider the candidate, I will normally agree to an interview. I can recall two situations, in fact, where such an approach has led me to hire the people in question.

> *It gives me great pleasure to converse with the aged. They have been over the road that all of us must travel and know where it is rough and difficult and where it is level and easy.*
>
> Plato (c.428–348 B.C.),
> Greek philosopher

SUMMARY

Remember that although you may be a little older than some others, you are probably more experienced and knowledgeable. Be aware of the qualities you have developed throughout your career that give you an advantage over younger workers.

• *Capitalize on your experience.* Inevitably you can demonstrate more experience than a younger worker can. Communicate your experiences to potential employers, focusing on those that are most relevant to the position.

- *Research and rehearse.* Before approaching a company, take time to do some research to determine the style of the company and rehearse questions you will pose in an interview.
- *Identify differentiators.* Identify a list of differentiators based on your life experience that will give you an advantage over younger workers.
- *Communicate positively.* Keep your nerves under control during an interview, and communicate openly and positively.
- *Align with your goals.* Ensure the position suits your desired work-life balance.
- *Listen carefully.* Listen carefully to what interviewers say. Don't be too focused on what you intend to say.
- *Take care with your personal presentation.* Pay attention to your personal presentation. Ask yourself whether you need to update your look to fit into a new environment.
- *Deal effectively with search and recruitment firms.* If you believe an intermediary such as a recruitment company is prejudiced against older workers, investigate other avenues for making direct contact with a potential employer, but do it carefully.

CHAPTER 6

Effective Career—and Life—Communication

B y this point in your life and your career, undoubtedly you've come to understand the value—make that the necessity—of clear and effective communication. You understand that it's not just what you say, but how and even when you say it that matter most.

But could it be that at this point in your career, you may no longer be as good a listener as you once were? Communication isn't a one-way process, after all. It's not just about talking, but about listening too. Effective communicating isn't merely sending information out in the general direction of someone's ears. It's about seeing that your information or opinion has been received, obtaining and interpreting a response, and repeating the process until agreement is reached or, at the very least, both parties have a clear understanding of what has been communicated.

When we're young and eager and starting out in a career, we tend to listen actively, even aggressively, looking for clues about how to succeed with this task, or how to gain the ear of that decision maker, or how to rise in the organization by acting one way or another. But as time passes and our own levels of experience and influence grow, a curious sense of deafness often sets in. We don't lose our talking skills, not by a long shot. It's our ability to listen that deteriorates. If you've ever left a meeting or appointment thinking, "He didn't hear a word I said," you've been subjected to the phenomenon.

> *A good listener is not only popular everywhere, but after a while he knows something.*
>
> Author unknown

Particularly if you are contemplating any type of change in your career, you'll need to be able to communicate well. Whether you're talking about long-term goals and needs with a friend or family member, interviewing a contact about conditions or opportunities in a new company or industry, or planning an active retirement, your ability to communicate effectively is likely to be put to the test as you ask for information, advice, and support. If you intend to keep on doing precisely what you've been doing for the next ten or twenty years, wouldn't this be a good time to assess, and if necessary regenerate, your business and personal communication skills?

I-SPEAK YOUR LANGUAGE

A number of years ago, to serve the needs of our clients at DBM, the company developed I-SPEAK Your Language, a system that we have found to be extremely useful for developing and maintaining strong communication skills. I-SPEAK, based on the theories of Swiss psychologist Carl Jung, looks at and interprets four major personality styles that individuals apply as they approach work and life: sensor, feeler, thinker, and intuitor, each associated with a fundamental behavioral function:

Style	Function
Sensor	Relates to experience through sensory perceptions
Feeler	Relates to experience through emotional reactions
Thinker	Analyzes, orders
Intuitor	Conceives, projects, induces

Rewired, Rehired, or Retired?

The premise is that most people have clear communication styles that can be understood relatively easily. The better our ability is to understand and respond to these styles, the more effective our communication is with others.

Sensors tend to be oriented to the present. They respond most immediately to things they can feel and touch, and tend to be detail oriented and realistic. They come across as doers. Feelers work off their emotions and gut feelings. They respond to human contact. Thinkers tend to be logical, systematic, structured people, oriented to data and information. Intuitors react to life by looking ahead to the future. They focus on making plans and setting goals.

Although each of us may favor one of the four primary I-SPEAK styles, no one relies on a single style in a vacuum. Most people blend all four styles together, with one or perhaps two styles being most prominent characteristically. If fact, if we place too much emphasis on a single style, we tend to find ourselves thinking in stereotypes. Still, if we can understand someone's dominant style, we can gain fascinating insight and clues about his or her likely actions and reactions.

DETERMINE YOUR OWN I-SPEAK STYLE

To help people understand their own I-SPEAK styles, DBM has created a self-test designed to reveal dominant communication styles.

Dominant Communication Styles Self-Test.

Each of the self-descriptive statements that follows has four different endings. Rank-order each ending, assigning:

4 to the statement that is most like you
3 to the statement that is next most like you
2 to the statement that is next most like you
1 to the statement that is least like you.

(Continued)

Dominant Communication Styles Self-Test. (Continued)

1. I am likely to impress others as:

    a. Practical and direct.

    b. Emotional and somewhat stimulating.

    c. Astute and logical.

    d. Intellectually oriented and difficult to understand.

2. When I work on a project, I:

    a. Want the project to be stimulating and involve lively interaction with others.

    b. Concentrate on making sure that the project is systematically or logically developed.

    c. Want to be sure that the project has a tangible benefit or outcome that will justify my spending time and energy on it.

    d. Am most concerned about whether the project is innovative or advances knowledge.

3. When I think about a problem at work, I usually:

    a. Think about concepts and relationships between events.

    b. Analyze what preceded the problem and what I plan next.

    c. Remain open and responsive to my feelings on the matter.

    d. Concentrate on reality—on things as they are right now.

4. When I am confronted by people with a different point of view, I can usually make progress by:

    a. Getting at least one or two specific commitments on which we can build later.

    b. Trying to put myself in someone else's place.

    c. Maintaining my composure and helping others see things simply and logically.

    d. Relying on my basic ability to conceptualize and pull ideas together.

Rewired, Rehired, or Retired?

5. In communicating with others, I may:

    a. Appear to lose interest with talk that is too detailed.

    b. Convey impatience with those who express ideas that are obviously incomplete.

    c. Show little interest in thoughts and ideas that show little or no originality.

    d. Usually ignore those who talk about the future, directing my attention to what needs to be done right now.

Now, to get an approximate indication of your primary I-SPEAK communication style, enter the number (1, 2, 3, or 4) you wrote next to each concluding statement.

	Intuitor	Thinker	Feeler	Sensor
1	d ____	c ____	b ____	a ____
2	d ____	b ____	a ____	c ____
3	a ____	b ____	c ____	d ____
4	d ____	c ____	b ____	a ____
5	c ____	b ____	a ____	d ____
Total				

Total each column. The column that has the highest total indicates your favored communication style. The column with the lowest total is your least-used style.

USING I-SPEAK IN ACTION

The more you understand the communication styles of the people around you, the more effectively you can communicate with them, making them more comfortable with you in the process and even improving your ability to influence them.

    The moment you enter someone's office or workspace, for example, you can begin to look for clues to communication styles. Look at the person's desk. A sensor's desk is likely to be cluttered and disordered. A feeler's desk may be covered with family photos, vacation souvenirs, a sports trophy, or other personal items. Thinkers usually keep their desks neat and orderly. An intuitor's desk is typically covered with books and reports.

A man hears only what he understands.

Author unknown

Scan the workspace itself. The sensor's office is likely to be a mess. If there is art on the wall, it's likely to be action oriented: a sailing scene perhaps. The feeler's office is personalized. The walls may be full of family pictures or company- or community-oriented items. The thinker's surroundings are usually neat and simple, even sterile. You may see charts on the walls. An intuitor's office may have abstract art on the wall, and the books scattered about are likely to have theoretical titles.

Finally, look for clues to communication styles when you begin to talk to someone. Sensors are likely to get down to business immediately and speak about problems and practical solutions. Feelers may begin conversations by talking about diverse topics—family, hobbies, the weather, vacations, even a new movie—and may digress from the conversation's central theme at any time. Thinkers talk about facts and figures. Intuitors may try to link your past to his or her future. Look for references to long-range goals and objectives.

REACTING EFFECTIVELY TO THE DIFFERENT I-SPEAK STYLES

When you have a good grasp of someone's communication style, you can tailor questions and responses accordingly. For instance, because time is very important to a sensor, don't ramble. You might begin the conversation by asking the sensor how much time he or she can spare. Sensors don't like introductions or historical background. Be concise, candid, and factual.

Feelers are interested in interpersonal relationships. If you find that you share a common family or community interest, mention this common ground. Don't be distracted or disturbed if your conversation goes off on a tangent. Also, although feelers often seem casual and informal,

Rewired, Rehired, or Retired?

don't interpret such behavior as the sign of a pushover. Feelers tend to be highly exacting.

Because thinkers respond to well-ordered data, stress facts and figures if you want to get your point across. It may help to lead the thinker step by step through your argument. Be specific and concise, and don't digress. Thinkers may seem aloof, but don't interpret that as indifference.

When you talk to an intuitor, stress the future. Ask questions about goals. Don't dwell on the past. Intuitors tend to place a premium on communication that is conceptual or philosophical. They tend to be impatient with details and are comfortable discussing a range of apparently disparate concepts at the same time.

UNDERSTANDING THE VALUE OF COMMUNICATION STYLES

The I-SPEAK styles are useful tools for effective communicating, but it is unwise to rely on them exclusively, for example, to reach an important conclusion on the basis of style alone. It is also important to understand that any style can be employed constructively or ineffectively. Intuitors can be original or unrealistic. Thinkers can be prudent or gun-shy. Feelers can draw out feelings in others, or they can incite conflicts. Sensors may be pragmatic or shortsighted.

The important point about these different styles isn't so much what type you are, but how effectively you can adapt your own style to the styles of people around you. Most of us are most receptive to messages that are delivered in a style similar to our own.

If you share the same style with the person you're communicating with, the process should be relatively straightforward. Just be yourself. But if you talk to people with other styles, the most effective communication is likely to result if you try to minimize the differences between your styles.

Try to present yourself in ways that complement the styles of others. If you want to communicate successfully, you need to translate your ideas into terms that the people who are listening to you can understand, accept, and ultimately act on. In essence, you need to speak their language.

INTERACTING WITH OTHER STYLES

Using I-SPEAK* to your advantage doesn't mean changing your own style or personality. It does mean gearing your comments to the situations and people around you.

If you are an intuitor, for example, a thinker may conclude that you are "far out" or too abstract and decide that you haven't backed up your points effectively. A feeler may find that you're too intellectual or theoretical. A sensor may decide that you're too idealistic.

If you are a thinker, an intuitor may determine that you lack vision and are overly cautious. A feeler may decide that you play things too safe and are bound by tradition. A sensor may conclude that you're too analytical and are unwilling to take action.

If you are a feeler, an intuitor may think that you worry too much. A thinker may decide that you are impulsive. A sensor may conclude that you're impractical.

If you're a sensor, an intuitor may decide that you tend to act before you think. A thinker may conclude that you lack depth. A feeler might find you insensitive.

It is possible to tailor your language to address such differences in style effectively. Suppose, for example, that you want to share this information: "I increased profits by cutting labor costs." Here is how you would present it to the different styles:

To a sensor: "The fastest way to get back into the black was to cut labor costs immediately."

To an intuitor: "Because I anticipated reduced sales, I planned a staggered reduction in the labor force, and that increased profits."

To a feeler: "There was no getting around the need to reduce labor costs, but I was careful to see that only people who were truly superfluous were affected. I also offered early retirement packages to those who were less than sure they wanted to stay."

---

*Drake Beam Morin, DBM, the DBM logo, and I-Speak are trademarks of Drake Beam Morin, Inc. Materials from "Satisfiers & Dissatisfiers" and "I-Speak Your Language" are used by permission. No permission to reprint these materials is otherwise granted.

To a thinker: "I identified a range of options to improve profits. After analyzing each alternative, it became clear that a workforce reduction was the best plan."

BE AN ACTIVE LISTENER

What we hear and observe is just as important as what we say. Although we may tend to think of effective communications in terms of our ability to talk to people convincingly, it's obviously just as important to be able to listen well too. Good communication is a two-way process.

Many of us are not natural listeners. We hear the things we say quite well, but we're not nearly as good at hearing and really understanding the words of others.

Poor listening is most often caused by not concentrating on what is being said. When you forget someone's name shortly after you've been introduced, for example, the chances are that you weren't concentrating on the name and storing it in your memory when it was being spoken.

Active listening—listening with concentration—is like any other skill: it can be learned and improved with practice. Perfecting this skill can help you interact more effectively with the people around you, both at work and in your life away from the job. Here are some simple techniques to improve your listening skills:

While the right to talk may be the beginning of freedom, the necessity of listening is what makes the right important.

Author unknown

- *Use restatement to check for understanding.* Restatement means rephrasing what you've already heard. When you restate in your own words something you've heard, you both internalize the message and check to see that you've received the information as the speaker intended it.

- *Focus on what people say as they are talking.* We often listen "faster" than we talk. Use the extra time to analyze not only the content but also the tone of the speaker.

> *You can tell more about a person by what he says about others than you can by what others say about him.*
>
> Author unknown

- *Maintain eye contact.* This sends the signal that you are interested in what others say to you and helps you maintain concentration on the message.

- *Use silence.* Your silence indicates that it is still the other person's turn to talk. People often offer additional information when you wait a moment to let them proceed.

- *Use nods and smiles.* In this way, you send the signal that you've heard what has been said and are interested in hearing more.

- *Complete other business before starting an important communication.* Make certain that you're not preoccupied with something other than the issue at hand.

- *Prepare your side of the conversation in advance.* This will leave you free to listen, because you won't have to worry about what you'll say next.

SUMMARY

It's not just what you say, but how and even when you say it that matters when it comes to clear and effective communication. Whether you're talking about long-term goals and needs with a friend or family member, talking to a contact about conditions or opportunities in a new company or industry, or planning an active retirement, your ability to communicate effectively is likely to be put to the test as you ask for information, advice, and support.

- *I-SPEAK Your Language.* I-SPEAK looks at and interprets four major personality styles that individuals apply as they approach work and life. The premise is that most people have clear communication styles that can be understood relatively easily. The better your ability is to understand and respond to these styles, the more effective your communication with others will be.

Rewired, Rehired, or Retired?

• *Determine your own I-SPEAK style.* To reveal your dominant communication style, identify which I-SPEAK style you most relate to. By completing the questions in the worksheet in this chapter, you will discover your most favored communication style and your least-used style.

• *Using I-SPEAK in action.* The more you understand the communication styles of the people around you, the more effectively you can communicate with them, making them more comfortable with you in the process and even improving your ability to influence them.

• *Reacting effectively to the different I-SPEAK styles.* When you have a good grasp of someone's communication style, you can tailor questions and responses accordingly.

• *Understanding the value of communication styles.* The important thing about understanding the different styles of communication isn't so much to identify what type you are, but how effectively you can adapt your own style to the styles of people around you. We tend to be most receptive to messages that are delivered in a style similar to our own.

• *Interacting with other styles.* Using I-SPEAK to your advantage doesn't mean changing your own style or personality. It does mean gearing your comments to the situations and people around you.

• *Be an active listener.* What we hear and observe is just as important as what we say. Good communication is a two-way process. Active listening—listening with concentration—is like any other skill: you can learn it and improve with practice. Perfecting this skill can help you interact more effectively with the people around you, both at work and in your life away from the job as well.

CHAPTER 7

How to Win When You Lose Your Job

Keep your face to the sunshine and you cannot see the shadow.
Helen Keller (1880–1968), American blind-deaf author, lecturer

A s we talk about charting a course and laying plans for the future, we need to remember that we can never be in complete control of our destiny. Remember all that change spinning around and through the universe? We're not immune to it, and it isn't always welcome. Given the changing nature of the workplace, in fact, losing a job at some point in a career may well be more a rule than an exception today. It isn't fun, of course, but it doesn't have to be a disaster.

THE REALITY CHECK

Losing a job can be a traumatic experience, particularly if you've worked with an organization for a lengthy period. The news may come as a complete surprise to you, or it may follow a period of uncertainty and stress. You may miss warning signs in any event, perhaps out of a comfortable, but no longer realistic, sense of job security. After working with one company for years, the concept of losing a job may seem inconceivable. But as we've learned, hard work, commitment, and loyalty to a company no longer ensure employment longevity.

One must never lose time in vainly regretting the past nor in complaining about the changes which cause us discomfort, for change is the very essence of life.

Jacques-Anatole François Thibault (1884–1924), French novelist and critic

Whatever the reason, the period following job loss can undoubtedly be one of the toughest interludes you may ever face. You may need to deal with a range of emotions: shock, confusion, anger, distrust, disappointment, and sadness. Regaining and maintaining your self-esteem in this difficult environment is of prime importance; the process frees you to move forward again.

Suddenly you are faced with sweeping changes and overwhelming concerns:

- Wondering what your friends and family will think of you
- Worrying about the loss of regular income
- Grieving over the need to leave long-term colleagues and friends
- Moving away from the familiar environment of your office
- Ceasing further involvement in projects already underway
- Losing the feeling and sense of identity of being part of a team
- Giving up perks and privileges: a company car, a space to park it in, an expense account
- Being cut off from established relationships with clients
- Disappearing from the invitation list for corporate functions
- Feeling uncomfortable in social settings where former colleagues may be present
- Losing the support of a personal assistant

For some people, losing a job is as tragic as ending a marriage or losing a family member. The fact that there may be no support structure in place to cushion the fall can make matters worse. You may not know who to talk to or where to turn. After all, you certainly didn't plan for things to turn out this way.

> Evidence of the cost imposed on men by leaving the workforce early is accumulating. In 1991, Dr Richard Smith, executive editor of the *British Medical Journal* said: "The evidence that unemployment kills—particularly in the middle age group—verges on the irrefutable."
>
> There is a 37% excess of mortality for unemployed men aged 45–55. For this group, losing their job is a major life event akin to losing a limb or a family member.
>
> Julie Macken, "Finished at 45," *Australian Financial Review,* July 11, 2000.

This could be the first time since the start of your career that you've really had to think about what to do next in your life or grapple with how to go about applying for a job, as you face the realization that tomorrow will be very different from yesterday.

If your employer provides outplacement counseling, you'll have some level of support in terms of what to do next, how to cope with your feelings, and how to create a plan for moving forward. But many people never get this support, and even those who do still need to deal with painful feelings.

How quickly the situation developed, and how well prepared or forewarned you were for it, will have a major impact on how quickly you recover. Many companies try to implement appropriate performance evaluation systems and strong communication channels to make employees aware of future employment uncertainty. Unfortunately, this is not always the case.

If you think you can, you can. If you think you can't you're right!

Mary Kay Ash (1915–2001), American businesswoman, founder of Mary Kay Cosmetics

> *It is not possible to shake hands properly with a clenched fist.*
>
> Author unknown

Throughout this period, it's essential to maintain a sense of perspective and proportion. Don't let the situation, no matter how grim it may appear, block out the light of reason. It's normal to question your abilities or wonder whether anyone will ever want—or hire—you again. Our brains tend to exaggerate negatives to the point of unclear resolution. Rather than slump into the depths of depression and low self-esteem, however, this is the time to focus on steps for regaining your self-esteem to achieve future career and life goals.

RESIST THE TEMPTATION TO REACT NEGATIVELY

Immediately following sudden job loss, you may feel the urge to lash out at the people or institution that placed you in this terribly uncomfortable position. Your common sense may be blurred by the onset of negative thoughts and feelings toward your previous employer. Don't let such emotions affect your decisions. This is the one time during the entire process of losing and then regaining a job when the best thing to do is nothing.

> *If you are patient in a moment of anger, you escape one hundred days of sorrow.*
>
> Chinese proverb

Future employment may understandably be foremost in your mind, but it's absolutely essential that you be in the right frame of mind before you even think about calling potential future employers or contacts in your industry. It is difficult to disguise the hurt immediately following job loss. It's highly likely that you'll come across as bitter, negative, or even desperate, so resist the temptation to call people immediately. Give yourself a couple of days or even a week to assess the impact of your situation before acting.

REBUILD YOUR SELF-ESTEEM

It's never easy for even the most confident among us to take rejection. People lacking in self-esteem often feel that the only way they can be successful and respected is for others to admire them. Although we should never place the value we have of ourselves in the hands of others, it's certainly understandable to feel concerned about how others will perceive the fact that we've lost our job.

Tradition dictates that we hold our heads high and avoid any display of inner emotions or torment. In this environment, people with low self-esteem become silent victims, too embarrassed to communicate their true feelings or seek support. Thankfully, however, this situation is changing.

> *Don't fix the blame, fix the problem.*
>
> Keith S. Pennington

It's becoming far more acceptable to acknowledge the pain of a difficult situation today. This isn't a license for self-pity, but a more realistic reaction to strong and genuine feelings.

To begin to feel like a winner again, focus on positive achievements and turn to your support network of friends and family. Here are some proven steps and considerations to help you regain self-esteem.

REVIEW PAST ACHIEVEMENTS

Consider your past achievements, whether they were personal, business, or public service, and review the ways in which you've had a positive impact on other people's lives.

Have you ever:

- Saved a person from an injury?
- Helped a friend make a tough decision?
- Developed a new idea that improved a business function?

> *The hopeful man sees*
> *success where others see*
> *failure, sunshine where*
> *others see shadows*
> *and storms.*
>
> O. S. Marden (1850–1924),
> American author

- Supported a friend or family member through a difficult time?
- Given a colleague a difficult task he or she succeeded in completing?
- Coached a team?
- Taken a risk with a business decision and have it pay off?
- Provided training or served as a mentor to others at work?
- Made a difference in someone's life?
- Made a recommendation that generated a cost saving?
- Won a major sale that provided work for many people?

Look closely at your achievements and recall what might have been the alternative had you not gotten involved. This may be a good time to revisit some of the probing questions contained in Chapter Three.

TURN TO FAMILY AND FRIENDS FOR SUPPORT

When our pride has been damaged and our self-esteem is low, we have a tendency to withdraw from family and friends, even though they are the very individuals who are most likely to want to help. We think, *Oh, I'd just be a burden.* If you find that you're limiting yourself to superficial conversations or declining offers of assistance to avoid losing face, it may be that you're working too hard to send the message, *Everything's just fine, thank you very much.*

Only you know to whom to turn and trust at this time, but doesn't it make sense that the people who really care about you are sure to want to go out of their way to help you? Keep in mind that you'll boost their own feelings of self-esteem by acknowledging that they're the ones you rely and depend on in difficult times.

Positive support and encouragement from friends make a huge difference. Any difficult situation will always be a shorter, less depressing, and less traumatic experience if you seek the support of friends.

Rewired, Rehired, or Retired?

Case Study: Who Cares? Your Real Friends and Family Do!

"Mike, you've contributed a lot to this organization, but we believe it's time for some fresh thinking and a more dynamic style of management."

What the hell does that mean? Mike thought. *That I'm a has-been at the age of fifty-four?*

After seven years as general manager of manufacturing of a large industrial company, Mike was devastated by the news. There were no warning signals, profits were at an all-time high, and to make matters worse, the devastating news was given to him by someone he considered a close friend.

He felt so humiliated that he actually felt ill, lost his appetite, and felt an uncontrollable longing to disappear. He seriously considered getting in his car and just driving thousands of miles away—he didn't care where—to escape the pain. His feelings resembled the emotions he felt when he'd lost his favorite uncle two years before. Mike was consumed by grief.

How could he possibly tell his family and friends he had lost the job he had been so proud of?

Mike didn't physically run away. What he did was put on an award-winning performance of continuing to work happily at his job for his final two weeks, keeping the news of his firing from even his wife of thirty-one years and his two teenage children.

Then he started a DBM outplacement program. In an initial conversation with his consultant, he broke down and sobbed that he felt too ashamed to tell his wife about his situation. Working closely with Mike for the next few days, the consultant convinced Mike to tell his wife what had happened. The release of sharing the news with her was phenomenal. She was incredibly supportive. Regrettably, however, Mike convinced her to withhold the news from their children or close friends. For two months, Mike and his wife lived in a vacuum, putting on a charade for their children and friends. The deception became more and more difficult to continue as Mike spent much of his time at home.

Discovering that Mike still had not told his children or friends, the DBM consultant suggested that Mike and his wife join him to discuss the situation.

The man who makes no mistakes does not usually make anything.

Edward John Phelps (1822–1900), American lawyer and diplomat

After an intense two-hour meeting, the consultant convinced them it would be better to share their burden with their children and friends.

After they did, the extraordinary amount of stress, distress, loss of sleep, and needless worry that Mike and his wife had endured suddenly dissipated. Mike realized he had been foolish. His children handled the situation with maturity and understanding, and the family's close friends provided enormous support. One friend provided Mike with a contact that ultimately led to a new job.

CONTROL THE IMPACT ON YOUR FAMILY

The loss of a job often leads to tension in the home, with parents sometimes trying to conceal the issues involved in a bid to protect their children. Aware of the tensions but without an explanation, children can be left confused and feel guilty that they are the cause of the tension. How you handle the situation can make a world of difference.

Case Study: Family Support Can Be a Powerful Force

Gary had just survived a round of retrenchments with his employer of almost thirty years when he chose to take a voluntary severance package. Excited by the prospect of a new start, the father of three calmly revealed his plan to his family. Although Gary felt the decision to be out of work for the first time in his life was risky, there was comfort in the fact that his wife, Joan, was also working full time.

For the first few months after he left his company, his daughters saw much more of their father than ever before, as he took the opportunity to do some repair work around the house while he looked for his ideal job. During this time, Gary grew closer to his children and felt more like a father than solely a breadwinner. He involved the family in his job search and kept the whole process open. Given that his daughters were on the brink of entering the workforce (both part time and full time), Gary wanted to make sure they understood that finding a job was very important.

After five months, Gary was offered a senior executive position with a major corporation. The position provided him with all the challenges he was seeking and the right cultural environment.

Gary credited the invaluable support from his family during this unsettling period in his life for helping him to secure a new position that was aligned with his competencies, goals, and personal values.

Children's reactions to a parent's job loss can have an adverse impact on the parent's job search, adding to the parent's trauma during this difficult time by producing feelings of inadequacy or failure. You can help your family understand your decision and situation and help to broaden their perspective on the world of work by being open:

- Give children information in digestible amounts, depending on their age.

- Explain how the job you did is no longer needed and is not a reflection of your personal values or performance.

- Explain that you will need their cooperation to help reduce unnecessary expenses.

- Give children space to ask their own questions.

- Remain calm, don't be defensive, and don't be critical when responding to their concerns.

- Where appropriate, give them things they can do to help, such as research on the Internet to assist your job search, and ask for their cooperation in being sensitive to your need for some peace and quiet if you are working from home.

- Always ensure that children see that you are in control of the situation, but don't be afraid to share your feelings when appropriate.

- Don't alarm children about the prospects of having to move to a new home or school unless and until it becomes a real possibility.

INVESTIGATE YOUR PASSIONS

Focusing on what you like doing and what you're good at helps you identify areas where you can achieve even greater success in the future. Take some time to think about your personal and professional likes and dislikes.

If one advances confidently in the direction of his dreams, and endeavors to live the life which he has imagined, he will meet with a success unexpected in common hours.

Henry David Thoreau
(1817–1862), American essayist,
writer, poet, naturalist

What are you really passionate about? Refer back to Chapter Three to review the things you genuinely enjoyed in your previous job—the aspects of work you absolutely loved and were passionate about. Review the things you disliked as well. Chances are that the elements of the job that you were passionate about are also the things you're really good at.

Don't fall into the trap of thinking about success exclusively in financial terms. If you identify and focus on areas you are passionate about, you may well find that you actually do very well financially by pursuing your likes, even though your initial main intention is not to maximize wealth. If you're passionate and focused, you will excel.

LOOK AND FEEL BETTER

Boost your self-esteem by achieving personal goals. This doesn't mean setting unrealistic objectives, like earning a spot in the next Olympics. But if you take the view that physical health assists mental health, then maintaining a fitness program that is in line with your age and general level of health can be valuable for many reasons.

Fitness and overall health contribute to your ability to focus. Both help to alleviate stress and tension. Of course, any proposed fitness regime should be discussed with your physician, but improving your fitness does-

Rewired, Rehired, or Retired?

n't have to mean researching complex physical fitness programs, going to the gym, or joining your local tennis club. It can mean, for example, taking a brisk walk several times a week.

Grey skies are just clouds passing over.

Duke Ellington (1899–1974), jazz musician

The impact of exercise may not be obvious at first, but after a few months, you'll find your mind is clearer, you'll sleep better at night, and you'll look and feel better. You may even start to receive compliments on your appearance. Your exercise program will improve the quality of your life, increase your motivation, and provide self-satisfaction by achieving the goals you've set for yourself.

A daily walk provides you with time to think about your situation and future. I always write down thoughts and inspirations that come to me during a walk as soon as I return home. You can be at your most creative during this time.

Walking provides you with the ideal opportunity to get out of your familiar environment each day so you don't remain at home. You may even be doing your partner a favor by providing him or her with some breathing space if your being around the house all the time is new.

CONSIDER NONPROFIT WORK

Getting involved with a nonprofit organization can refocus your energies away from the negative aspects of job loss, enabling you to provide support in new areas and lifting your own sense of value and self-worth in the process.

Nonprofits welcome the support of professionals who are able to donate their services to a cause they find important. Many of these organizations are starved for funding and experience limited growth as a result. The people who work for them are

When nothing is sure, everything is possible.

Margaret Drabble (1939–), British novelist

> *I firmly believe that if you follow a path that interests you, you'll be a person worthy of your own respect.*
>
> Neil Simon (1927–), playwright

typically extremely committed and hard-working individuals who are passionate about the causes they serve.

Moving into this environment and working with such people on a part-time basis, particularly during career transition, can help you gain an understanding of a different way of life. In your previous job, you may have worked long hours, earning a very good income and focusing narrowly on advancing your career to the next level.

Nonprofit organizations you are already familiar with could include your church, local charitable groups, your college, sporting clubs, a retirement home, or an environmental group. Perhaps you feel passionate about helping a particular charity that is close to your heart. Why not pick up the telephone to find out how you can help? Although you may not be paid for your services, you will be giving to others.

Becoming involved with a nonprofit organization could change your outlook on life. It's sure to expand your network, give you a feeling of being part of a valuable team, and allow you to make a real contribution to a worthy cause. Successful experiences make you feel like a winner.

THINK LIKE A WINNER

Thinking like a winner is not easy soon after losing a job. But remember the old question: Is the glass half full or half empty? It comes down to the way you look at a situation. If you think positively about yourself, others, and the world around you, the world often meets your expectations, and you can achieve your personal and professional goals.

> *Would it be possible to win if you couldn't lose?"*
>
> Jim Rohn, philosopher

Look at the familiar example of a team on a losing streak. The players probably still have the skills to win, but they may not be pushing themselves hard enough because they've lost the feeling of winning. Often, it's the mind games that people on a losing team play on themselves that prevent them from becoming a winning team.

Winners do tend to be cheerful. No matter how dark the situation seems to be, raising your sights, being persistent, acknowledging the possibilities, and staying positively focused can help you achieve your goals. So think and act like a winner. This means focusing on tomorrow, not yesterday:

- Yesterday you lost your job and all the benefits that went with it. Remember that you can't change what happened.
- Yesterday you were bitter about the way you were treated.
- Yesterday your boss was your friend.
- Yesterday the company was stupid to let you go.

Face the facts. You can't change the past. It has happened, and that's that. You will go forward only if you focus positively on tomorrow. Success will be reflected in everything you do: the way you handle an interview, the way you communicate with friends and family, and the way you make decisions.

When interviewing, I am instantly turned off by people who complain about a previous employer or make nothing but negative, caustic statements. This sort of negativity can be poisonous to an organization and to your own employment chances.

It's time to get on with getting on. As hard as it may be, tomorrow is a new day in a new life in a new world. It's always difficult at first, but then you will start to realize that you still have many reasons to smile. Think about the successful people

> *To be a great champion you must believe you are the best. If you're not, pretend you are.*
>
> Muhammad Ali (1942–),
> world champion
> heavyweight boxer

you know. Chances are they feel good about themselves because they think they are winners.

COMMUNICATE POSITIVELY

To recover successfully from losing your job, you need to enlist a positive outlook. Nurturing a positive frame of mind helps you to gain control of your future and create your own destiny.

Although it can be extremely difficult, aim to communicate in a positive, respectful manner at all times. When dealing with pressure, it's so easy to take our frustrations out on others. The key is to control your reactions so that you communicate positively, and therefore effectively, without offending anyone or regretting your words later. Communicating with negative undertones can poison our frame of mind. Positive communication not only makes people feel better about themselves, but it also increases our own self-worth.

What you say can be less important than how you say it. Take time to think about communicating positively to others before you speak. Show an interest in the people you meet. Look at the world anew.

Case Study: Communicate to Motivate

A friend recently experienced the importance of a positive communication style when he was named CEO of a company. For many years, he had worked as the finance director, successfully controlling capital expenditures and ensuring that profit and loss accounts were completed on time. He did so well that he was considered for promotion to the role of CEO. But in his role as finance director, he had developed a style of negative communication: "You've overspent your budget!" "These accounts do not reconcile!" "Why wasn't that report ready on time?"

This style of communication was not as effective following his promotion to CEO. He continued to talk to people within the organization with a similar negative approach: "You haven't achieved your sales budget" "Don't build the product mix until you have the costs in order!"

110

The message was clear. He had to change his communication style if he wanted to succeed in his new position. Good leaders inspire their staff by motivation and encouragement rather than admonishment. Successful people start each sentence with a positive statement. My friend worked to change his style, saying things like, "You've really made great progress in building up the business. Is there any way I can help you lift the sales in your division?" and "I can see you're working to improve performance. What assistance can I provide with training?"

Although it took a lot of practice in his new role, he persisted and finally succeeded.

Just as this finance director did when he changed his focus on being named CEO, you can have an amazing impact on everyone around you by starting each sentence with a positive statement.

It is not in the stars that hold our destiny but ourselves.

William Shakespeare
(1564–1616), British playwright,
poet, actor

If you diligently practice and make sure you communicate positively with others, it will start to come naturally within about two weeks. You will be clearly looking for positives rather than negatives. You'll start to believe in positive outcomes and start to believe in your own voice because of the impact you are having on others.

DON'T RESIST CHANGE

Resistance to change is common following job loss. But you must overcome it so that you can take the positive steps that will lead you into the next phase of your life.

Don't expect to cope with the changes in both your career and personal life immediately. After a week or two, you may respond better to your new circumstances. Still, there are likely to be other times where

When one door closes, another opens; but we often look so regretfully upon the closed door, that we do not see the one which has opened for us.

Alexander Graham Bell
(1847–1922),
inventor of the telephone

You can't climb a smooth mountain.

C. I. Dixon

change feels like an obstacle: pursuing a job search, for example, entering a new work environment, meeting new people, and establishing new priorities. You need to respond to your new circumstances and equate change with opportunity.

YOUR LIFE IS YOUR DECISION

Losing your job gives you the opportunity to identify what is important to you and move forward in the direction of your choice. The loss of a job usually isn't your decision, of course, but it can give you precious time to reevaluate your priorities in life and take control of your future.

SUMMARY

Recognize the changes that will become effective following job loss:

• *The reality check.* The feelings that you may experience can be wide-ranging and possibly traumatic. Maintain a sense of perspective and proportion to ensure that these problems and setbacks don't block out the light of reason.

• *Resist the temptation to react negatively.* Your mental clarity may be blurred and accompanied by the onset of negative feelings toward your previous employer. Allow yourself time to come to terms with your situation.

- *Rebuild your self-esteem.* You are facing overwhelming changes and concerns in your life when a job is taken from you. Start to focus on positive achievements, and turn to your support network for assistance.

- *Review past achievements.* Reflect on how you have had a positive impact on other people's lives. Use your reflection to realize just how special you are.

- *Turn to family and friends for support.* Remember that it's your friends and family who care the most, want to help, and usually have the most to offer. Let them.

- *Control the impact on your family.* The loss of a job can create tension in the home, with parents sometimes trying to conceal the issues in an effort to protect their children. If not managed properly, children's reactions can have an adverse impact on the parent's job search, adding to the parent's trauma during this difficult time by producing feelings of inadequacy or failure.

- *Investigate your passions.* Take time to consider what you really like and dislike. You'll discover the elements of the job you were passionate about and would like to continue to focus on in the future. When you are passionate and focused, you put yourself in a position to excel. Life's rewards are likely to follow.

- *Look and feel better.* Maintain your physical fitness. Good health and fitness contribute to your ability to focus and can alleviate stress and tension.

- *Consider nonprofit work.* You have an opportunity to give to others, and the period of job loss can be a time to keep you active while you contribute to something outside, and larger than, yourself. This may give you a different outlook about what you really want to do in the future. In any case, a successful experience will make you feel like a winner.

- *Think like a winner.* When you do, you will be one. If we think positively about ourselves, others, and the world around us, the world more often meets our expectations. Focus on tomorrow and boost your self-esteem.

- *Communicate positively.* Act and react positively toward others at all times. Remember that what you say can be less important than the way you say it. Look at the world with fresh eyes. If you work diligently and practice communicating positively with others, it will come naturally. Optimism is habit forming, and it's a nice habit to have.
- *Don't resist change.* The world is changing constantly, and change affects all of us in different ways. Respond to your new circumstances by equating change with opportunity.
- *Your life is your decision.* Whatever your next step may be, whether to pursue further employment in a similar role, make a career change, work for yourself, undertake further education, or retire, you are now in a position to assume control over your life and career.

CHAPTER 8

Networking

When spider webs unite, they can tie up a lion.
Ethiopian proverb

In this rapidly changing world of work, one truth remains constant: the unquestionable value of networking. Establishing, maintaining, and expanding a network of contacts is the most valuable career management activity you can undertake. The value is not limited to finding a job, so don't think of networking as a job search tool exclusively. It's a career—and even a life—resource. Networking does lead to employment opportunities, of course, but it can also do much more than that. If you'd like to secure a promotion or are considering a lateral move in the organization you work for, your network can point you in the right direction. If you're thinking about changing companies or are attracted to the idea of an entirely new career, networking can help you assemble information, narrow your choices, and connect with people who can assist and support your activities. Are you giving thought to retirement? Test your ideas with members of your network.

> *Long-range planning does not deal with future decisions, but with the future of present decisions*
>
> Peter Drucker (1909–),
> American management
> consultant and author

Networking allows you to reestablish contact with old acquaintances as well as meet new people. Even when contacts are unable to provide direct assistance or information, they still become members of your ongoing informational network and are valuable as potential sources of future referrals. Networking is a powerful technique that requires research, planning, and practice to use effectively.

NETWORKING IS A TWO-WAY PROCESS

As you develop and take advantage of your network, don't think of yourself as a beggar asking for favors. The people you talk to may themselves learn and benefit from your ideas. Most of them will appreciate being asked for assistance and will be happy to help. It's natural for most of us to want to help others. Many contacts will feel pleased with themselves for being able to assist and for being considered a so-called expert. I tend to feel honored when someone values my advice enough to ask for my help.

Be civil to all; sociable to many; familiar with few; friend to one; enemy to none.

Benjamin Franklin (1706–1790), American scientist, publisher, diplomat

Also, consider the one-good-turn-deserves-another school of thought. When you enlist people in your network, you become a member of their networks in return, a source of assistance should they need it in the future. Think about experiences when you have willingly provided assistance to people who have asked for your help. You probably wanted to help, but you may also have realized that there could come a time when you might seek their assistance in return.

It is rarely a waste of time to discuss your plans or needs with others, because it's usually impossible to anticipate who will be most helpful. In these days of ongoing change in employment, you can never be sure who will be able to assist you or whom you will be able to assist in the future.

Rewired, Rehired, or Retired?

WHO IS IN YOUR NETWORK?

The networking process begins with identifying contacts. Sometimes we think of our network as a narrow band of colleagues and customers. But if you've lived in the same community for more than two years, it is quite likely your valuable network exceeds a hundred people. Do you sing in a church choir? All of its members are potential network members. Do you coach a youth soccer team on weekends? Think of all those parents. Have you visited your dentist recently? Think of all the contacts he or she might refer you to.

Remember this: most people want to help, so don't be shy. And even if you do feel shy, consider the opportunity. Research conducted by DBM has consistently found that most people secure new positions through networking. This statistic holds true across different countries and cultures.

All life form seems to be driven by instinct and the genetic code except for humans. Only humans can greatly alter the course of their life and arrive at a different destination.

Jim Rohn,
American businessman,
author, philosopher

Recognize who actually contributes to your network. Using the Network Contacts worksheet, start to make a list of the contacts you have.

Always continue to add layers to your network. Each new person you meet is likely to be able to introduce you to another new circle of contacts. By continuing to expand your network, additional opportunities become available. The more people you contact, the more introductions you will achieve so that your skills, interests, and availability become known to a larger group.

As your network grows, don't lose control of it. Keep a record of each member, contact details, current employment information for that person, and details of your last communication.

Network Contacts.

1. Work colleagues: Whom have you worked with over the past ten years? In particular, think about superiors, peers, and subordinates with whom you had a positive relationship.

2. Customers: What customers or clients have you had a close relationship with over the past ten years? Pull together a list of the top five from each of your three most recent jobs (different jobs in one company or in different companies).

3. Suppliers: Who supplied goods or services to your business or home that you have had an active and positive relationship with over the past ten years? If they've supplied you in the past, there is a good chance that they will want to supply you again in the future.

4. Support service providers: Who has provided professional services to you personally or your organization? Include accountants, lawyers, realtors, and other major service providers. Don't forget search firms if you've used them on the job.

Network Contacts. (Continued)

5. Sporting contacts: Consider people you know well in any local sports or athletic club that you or your children have been involved with. Former teammates could prove to be worthwhile contacts.

6. Local business owners: With whom have you established friendly relationships in your local area?

7. Social and church contacts: Is there someone from a local church, synagogue, or social club who can provide assistance?

8. Family: The people who care most about you are often never asked to help. Don't forget that family contacts extend to relatives of your partner or spouse.

9. Friends: We often exclude friends who naturally want to help us, because we worry that we will be intruding on the friendship. But what's a friendship for if not to help? Surely you would want to help your friends if they could benefit from your assistance.

(Continued)

Network Contacts. (Continued)

10. Retired people: Retirees are often eager to assist. People who have been successful and respected throughout their business lives often maintain associations and contacts well into retirement. It is surprising how often they are not contacted, however; people assume that because they are no longer actively involved in business, they won't be much help. Make no such assumptions.

11. Neighbors: What do your neighbors do? Do they have relevant contacts?

12. Parents of your children's friends: What business are they in? Can they provide assistance?

13. Professional associations: Think about contacts you have in professional associations. You may also have contacts you haven't thought about in a trade organization, business club, or other professional group.

14. College and university alumni associations: These associations often have career networks available to assist you with your job search.

People regularly tell me, "I just don't know enough people well to build a decent network." By giving careful consideration to the list in the worksheet, it will become obvious that virtually anyone can easily develop a list of a hundred contacts or more.

When you reach for the stars, you may not quite get them, but you won't come up with a handful of mud either.

Leo Burnett,
American marketing expert

Case Study: The True Power of Networking

Michael is a successful international businessman in his late forties. He specializes in marketing and management in the pharmaceutical industry and has lived and worked in the United Kingdom, New Zealand, Switzerland, the Arabian Gulf, and Taiwan. Michael, his wife, Judy, and their two-year-old daughter were living in Taipei when the multinational pharmaceutical company he worked for merged with another company and downsized significantly. Michael's position was eliminated.

After careful consideration, the family decided they would like to live in Australia. Michael began his outplacement program in Hong Kong and then transferred to the Sydney DBM office to continue his job search. Because neither Michael nor Judy had ever lived in Australia before, the process was going to be even more challenging. They didn't know anyone in Australia and therefore didn't have the security of an established support network of friends and business colleagues. Michael had no alternative but to make cold calls.

He researched the market thoroughly to identify target companies throughout Australia with which he would like to work. He mailed more than a hundred marketing letters, followed up with telephone calls, and then proceeded to attend numerous interviews. In essence, Michael was establishing a network of contacts that would eventually lead him to a position with an employer of his choice.

By the time Michael was offered and accepted a position with a major international company, he had contemplated nineteen different opportunities at various stages.

The entire process took only three months. It certainly shows how powerful networking can be.

FOCUS ON EFFECTIVE COMMUNICATION

As you build and use your network, don't rush off and approach everyone you know. Be selective; identify what you want to achieve. If you're targeting a job in the local community, the people who can help most are likely to be different from those you would approach if you were seeking a job with a major national or international company.

Remember that your initial approach with any contact is likely to have an enormous impact and may well determine whether the individual will want to help you in the future. Think ahead. Work out what you want to achieve, and then develop an approach that won't put your contact into a difficult or uncomfortable situation.

You don't stumble into the future. You create your own future.

Roger Smith,
American businessman

For example, if you approached a man in your personal network, told him you were seeking employment, and wondered if he had anything available within his company, you would most likely put him in an uncomfortable position. He probably wouldn't want to offend you, however, and so he might find it difficult to say no. Instead, he could say, "Let me get back to you." Later, when he hasn't called, you find that he always seems to be unavailable when you try to contact him. The following conversation might produce a more effective result: "You're familiar with my background and experience. I'm looking for another role using my skills in the same industry sector across the country. I'd really appreciate your advice. Do you think I should contact Company X? Where else might I look for possible opportunities?"

Develop a script to help you cover all the points you want to make in an initial communication. Practice your script until you are convinced that you're coming across in the right manner: friendly, not pushy.

The result of this type of communication is that you have indicated to a potentially valuable contact that you are in the job market without directly asking about opportunities within his or her company. You haven't asked for a job, so no one is under pressure to say no. If there is an available position that may be suited to your skills and experience, your contact can explore exactly what you are looking for in greater detail.

The other benefit that emerges from taking an indirect approach is that most people are willing to give you names of contacts if you have a positive relationship with them. They will often telephone a colleague on your behalf, a sure way to open doors. These types of referrals from well-respected people in your industry can have enormous impact in terms of getting you in the door for the next meeting. Still, as you move from contact to contact, be sure you have clearance to use someone's name to establish contact with someone new. Be sensitive to the fact that you are representing another person when you use his or her contacts.

It is not wise to ask directly for a job when first approaching your network. Always ask for suggestions. And don't ask for favors. Ask for advice.

SUCCEED THROUGH NETWORKING

In the consulting business that I developed, every lead for new business came from a current client, a known contact, a referral, or someone who

Everything comes to him who hustles while he waits.

Thomas Alva Edison (1847–1931), American inventor, entrepreneur, founder of General Electric

Don't be afraid to take a big jump. You can't cross a chasm in two small steps.

David Lloyd George (1863–1945),
British prime minister

has had direct contact with the company. We are constantly using our network to develop new business.

The more contacts you make, the greater is the possibility that someone will contact you when a potentially suitable position becomes available. The value of networking is that you are constantly advertising yourself. Networking enables you to have access to jobs before they are advertised. Networking means you describe what it is that you're looking for rather than trying to fit into someone else's job specification.

SUMMARY

Establishing, maintaining, and expanding your network of contacts are vital for effectively managing your career and life. Networking leads to opportunities. Realize the value of networking. Networking can help you connect with people who can assist you and support your goals. Even when contacts are unable to provide direct assistance or information, they still become members of an ongoing information network.

• *Networking is a two-way process.* The people you contact for assistance may one day require assistance from you. Most people will feel flattered you have contacted them.

• *Who is in your network?* Identify who contributes to your network. Your contacts across all facets of life are valuable resources because they have formed a positive opinion about you, either socially or in business.

• *Focus on effective communication.* Be sensitive when using someone's name to establish a contact, and always make sure that your first approach to someone in your network be the product of careful planning. Never ask directly for a job. Always ask for suggestions. Don't ask for favors. Always ask for advice.

• *Succeed through networking.* Remember that the more contacts you make, the greater is the possibility that someone will contact you when a potentially suitable position becomes available.

124

CHAPTER 9

Overcoming Phone Phobia

Life shrinks or expands in proportion to one's courage.
Anaïs Nin (1914–1977), French-born American novelist and dancer

Most of us resist change as a matter of course, preferring to remain in a stable and predictable environment or even longing for the "good old days" (without realizing, perhaps, that turning back the clock would itself be a highly significant form of change). But however natural it may be to try to defy change, it isn't realistic, since reality means change. And when it comes to our careers, reality means that there is no such thing as an employment situation that remains constant. As a result, the more we focus on moving forward within a changing world, the more successful we are sure to be.

Moving forward often means thinking about or actually pursuing a new job. To do that, we need to think like salespeople and sell ourselves. Anyone can write a good resumé these days, but how can we make ourselves stand out from the pack?

ASSESSING YOUR LEVEL OF PHONE PHOBIA

The best place to stand out is in a face-to-face meeting with someone, typically achieved by making initial contact over the telephone. That is not always a comfortable process. Picking up the phone to talk to someone you

> *Courage is not the absence of fear; it is the making of action in spite of fear, the moving out against the resistance engendered by fear into the unknown and into the future.*[*]
>
> M. Scott Peck (1936–),
> American psychologist and author

have never spoken to before can be difficult, especially if the person does not seem as interested or as responsive to your call as you would like. It may have nothing to do with you, of course: your contact could be late for a meeting, or thinking deep thoughts, or recovering from the flu for that matter. But whatever the reason, it's up to you to overcome your phone phobia if you wish to achieve your goals.

The goal of the phone call is not to get a job but to get in the door to sell your skills and experience so that you might be offered a job. You don't want to use up all your ammunition on the phone, of course. But if you can't reach the point where you are face to face, how will potential employers or clients know how good you are?

REASONS FOR PHONE PHOBIA

There are a myriad of reasons we use to talk ourselves out of making a call when it comes to promoting ourselves or when job prospecting. In most cases, however, once we have found the courage to pick up the phone and make the call, we realize it wasn't nearly half as bad as we had anticipated or imagined it may be.

> *It is better to live one day as a lion than a hundred years as a sheep.*
>
> Motto on Italian twenty lire coin

There is always a possibility of rejection or failure, yet without your initiating discussion or debate and taking a chance, you will never know whether the opportunity existed for you to achieve the goal and the success you desire.

[*]Reprinted with the permission of Simon & Schuster from THE ROAD LESS TRAVELED by M. Scott Peck, M.D. Copyright © 1978 by M. Scott Peck.

Assessing Your Level of Call Reluctance!®

To get a sense of your level of call reluctance®, check "Yes" or "No" in the columns to the right of each statement:*

                                                     Yes   **No**

- I spend more time planning to promote myself than actually doing it.

- I'm not really trying to promote myself as much as I could or should, because I'm not sure it's worth the hassle anymore.

- I don't try as much as I could or should to initiate contact with influential people in my community who could be prospects for my future.

- I tend to get really uncomfortable when I have to call people on the telephone I don't know, who aren't expecting my call, to ask them to do something they may not want to do.

- I think that having to call people I don't know, and who are not expecting my call, is demeaning.

- Self-promotion doesn't really bother me. I just don't apply myself to it very purposefully.

- I would avoid giving a presentation to a group if I could.

- Actually, prospecting doesn't really bother me. I could initiate more contacts if I were not involved in so many other activities.

- I have clear goals, and I like to talk about them. In fact, I probably spend more time talking about them than working toward them.

(Continued)

Assessing Your Level of Call Reluctance!® (Continued)

Yes   No

- I need time to psych myself up before I can prospect.

- I tend to spend a lot of time shuffling, planning, prioritizing, and organizing the names on my prospecting list before I actually put them to use.

- Making cold calls is difficult for me.

- I tend to feel somewhat uneasy when I self-promote, because deep down, I probably feel that promoting yourself is not really respectable or proper.

- To me, making sales presentations to my friends is unacceptable, because it would look as if I was trying to exploit a friendship.

- I often feel as if I am intruding on people when I prospect.

- Making a sales presentation to members of my own family is out of bounds: it might look as if I was trying to exploit my relatives.

- It is very important to me to find innovative, alternative ways to prospect and self-promote that are more dignified than the methods other people use.

128

	Yes	No

- I think that prospecting probably takes more out of me emotionally than other people.

- I would probably do all right one-on-one, but I would get pretty nervous if I found out that I had to make a presentation to a large group of people.

- Highly educated professional people like lawyers and doctors tend to annoy me, so I don't try to initiate contact with them, even though I probably could if I wanted to.

Total

Total Yes Answers	Interpretation
1–2	Either you are experiencing no difficulty associated with prospecting (self-promotion) at the present time, or you are having trouble but don't want to reveal how much.
3–4	You are like most other people. The fear of self-promotion is present but only in nontoxic amounts. It may be occasionally annoying, but it is not likely to be serious if it remains at this level. It should be manageable by simply emphasizing the markets and prospecting techniques you are most comfortable with and avoiding those that make you uncomfortable.
5–6	You have moderate levels of call reluctance®. The fear of self-promotion is limiting your prospecting to a level below your ability. Your prospecting is probably out of sync with your market potential.
7–8	You exhibit a considerable amount of call reluctance®. Your prospecting is probably a shadow of what it could or needs to be.
9 or more	You have a great deal of difficulty making calls and need to develop these skills aggressively if you want to achieve your career goals.

*This information is based on the "Call Reluctance® Self-Rating Scale" from *The Psychology of Sales Call Reluctance* by George W. Dudley and Shannon L. Goodson, 1999. Call Reluctance® is a registered trademark of Behavioral Sciences Research Press, Inc., Dallas, Texas USA. ALL RIGHTS RESERVED.

> *I have learned over the years that when one's mind is made up, this diminishes fear; knowing what must be done does away with fear.*
>
> Rosa Parks (1913–),
> American civil rights activist

It is therefore important to understand the common causes for phone phobia and identify which cause is most likely to interfere with your personal job prospecting. Phone phobia can stem from a number of reasons:

• A lack of experience in initiating contact with strangers

• Your cultural heritage

• A reluctance to bother friends

• Not wanting to approach family members in case they think less of you

• Being intimidated by the seniority of the person you need to contact

• Not wanting to be viewed as having to beg for a favor, a position that you may consider socially unacceptable

By overcoming your phone phobia, you will discover you have more opportunities to say the right things to the right people to pursue your path to future success.

WHAT'S THE WORST THAT CAN HAPPEN?

Sometimes fear of the unknown can cause you to delay in making a call. If that is the case, consider the worst that someone you phone or visit—a prospective employer, recruitment firm, contact, or even a close friend—to gather information or undertake a job search can do in response to your inquiry:

• Refuse to take your call?

• Slam down the phone?

• Rant and rave?

• Abuse you verbally?

• Embarrass you?

130

- Endanger your social status?
- Make you a laughing stock?

Even in the unlikely event that you suffer this sort of response, remember that it honestly may not be anything personal. You may have called someone at an inconvenient time, or your contact may be having a particularly bad day. And, in any case, if people are rude or offensive by nature, doesn't that say more about them than it does about you?

> *No one can make you inferior without your consent.*
>
> Eleanor Roosevelt (1884–1962),
> American first lady,
> lecturer, humanitarian

The important point to remember is that if you make no calls, you gain zero opportunities. If you make twenty calls, zero opportunities are still a possibility, but how many opportunities might you have? Maybe only a few—or maybe a whole lot—but you will certainly be well ahead of taking no action at all.

The underlying message is that if you don't ask, you don't get. If you approach twenty people, it's unlikely that you'll be successful twenty times. But whether you get rejected by five, ten, fifteen, or even twenty of these people, unless you ask, you'll never know.

Some of the people you contact may want to assist you for reasons of self-preservation. After all, there's always the possibility that they could be asking the same of you in the not-too-distant future. Or the person you contact may simply want to return a favor you've done in the past.

Remember that fear of failure and rejection inhibit peak performance. When you don't achieve success, it's not a mistake; it's a learning experience. Successful experiences make you feel like a winner. Give it a try. You have very little to lose.

> *While one person hesitates because he feels inferior, the other is busy making mistakes and becoming superior.*
>
> Henry C. Link

REMEMBER FRIENDS AND FAMILY

Often we do not turn to those who want to help us the most: our family and close friends. They are the ones who are likely to have the most to gain or lose, as they legitimately care about us. Families are eternal.

Genuine friends also really want to help. I have a friend who was going through a difficult time in business, which put him under severe financial and emotional pressure. Other friends and I approached him to offer help, but he always said he was fine. The pressure increased, and he was obviously handling it with difficulty, but still he insisted he didn't want help. The crazy reality is that often those we regard as good friends feel helpless, when they would be only too happy to help if we simply asked them.

A ship in port is safe, but that is not what ships are built for.

Benazir Bhutto (1953–), former prime minister of Pakistan

Some people find it is easier to call on behalf of someone else than for themselves. For example, how difficult would it be for you to call someone to say that a friend is very skilled, very experienced, and worth looking at for a job? How difficult would it be for you to do the same for yourself? Why? Is your friend more skilled than you are? Are you intimidated or do you fear rejection?

MAKING A SUCCESSFUL PHONE CALL

To make a successful phone call, you need to be motivated, and you need goals. Who is your target? What is your strategy? What do you want from the call?

What you say to yourself about prospecting has a powerful impact on what you feel and how you act when prospecting. You need to think like a salesperson and sell yourself.

It's worth noting some simple tips for preparing for and making the actual call to assist you in overcoming phone phobia:

Rewired, Rehired, or Retired?

- Be focused and determined. Concentrate on the task at hand.

- Plan carefully. Have a list of points you wish to cover during the call.

- Have a clear goal. What is your motivation? Think about what you want to achieve from the call. You want to win! You want to arrange a face-to-face interview. Ultimately, it can lead to your obtaining a fulfilling job and personal or financial rewards.

- Develop a minimum goal of what you want to achieve from the phone call. Is it a meeting with the person you're calling? A reference? The names of two other people to call?

- Visualize your goals. It works with world-class athletes. Your thoughts can determine your future. Think of the feeling you'll have when you've made the call and achieved your goals: the adrenaline rush, the empowerment, the energy. It's good to be a dreamer.

- Boost your confidence before you call. Make a list of five to ten positive thoughts about yourself, and refer to them before you dial. Even the process of developing the list will help. Here are some examples:

  I'm smart.

  I'm determined and persistent.

  I'm caring and thoughtful.

  I'm reliable and dependable.

  I'm loyal.

  I've already achieved a lot in my career.

- Prepare a script. There's nothing wrong with having a script in front of you when you're on the telephone. Just make sure you don't sound as

> *The follies which a man regrets most in his life are those which he didn't commit when he had the opportunity.*
>
> Helen Rowland (1875–1950),
> American journalist

if you're reading the words, and be prepared to go off the script if that's the direction the discussion takes. Your script doesn't have to be developed word for word; bulleted points will do. But it does help to have something in front of you listing your key thoughts. After four or five calls, your script will become second nature.

- Don't say too much on the phone. Leave the individual curious to find out more face to face. This is where a script can be particularly useful because it helps you determine what to say and what to save.

- Be sure you are in the right frame of mind and environment prior to the call. Sit up straight. Have a glass of water handy. Call from a quiet place where there are no distractions.

- Think positively. If you're not in a positive frame of mind, go for a walk beforehand to collect your thoughts and clear your mind.

- If you don't really want the job, don't call. Be honest with yourself.

- Read the person. If the person sounds busy, ask if there is a better time to call.

- Don't be afraid to ask questions. By asking well-thought-out questions, you demonstrate that you know what you're talking about.

Never bend your head. Always hold it high. Look the world straight in the eye.

Helen Keller (1880–1968), American blind-deaf author, lecturer

- Try not to talk too fast. Although you may be nervous, the person you are calling doesn't have to be aware of this. Talking too fast and not enunciating properly can suggest that you are nervous.

- Smile when you speak. This sounds like an odd suggestion for a phone call, but it's amazing the difference it can make. Try smiling while speaking in front of a mirror, and notice the improvement in your voice.

- Listen carefully and take notes. Make sure you listen to what the person on the other end of the line is saying. Sometimes nerves can blur your memory, so writing key points down during the call can help you focus.

134

- Is the position or opportunity with this person or company right for you? Does the company provide a high self-esteem environment? Unless you are desperate for employment you usually have a choice.

PICK UP THE PHONE

The sooner you start making calls, the more experienced you'll become and the easier the process will be. Overcoming phone phobia can be difficult, but it is certainly achievable. If you want to arrange an interview and pursue a particular career direction with a company, you simply have to make an initial call. Writing letters or sending e-mails alone will not give the person you are communicating with a chance to know you.

Begin with the big picture. Start to think about your role in life and what you want to achieve from now on. If it's honestly important to you and perhaps to your family as well, how hard can it be to make a phone call? As you know if you've ever sold an idea, product, or service, it is very hard to sell anything unless you believe it is the best.

I wouldn't be able to sell the services of DBM unless I believed it was the best outplacement and career management company with the best consultants, the best support materials, the best training, and the people with the greatest commitment to helping people get suitable new jobs. If I didn't believe that, I wouldn't be with DBM.

> The thick-skinned fearlessness expected in sales people is more fiction than fact. It turns out that many sales people are struggling with a bone-shaking fear of prospecting. This fear tends to persist regardless of what they sell, how well they have been trained to sell it, or how much they personally believe in the product's worth.
>
> George W. Dudley and Shannon L. Goodson,
> *The Psychology of Sales Call Reluctance* (1999)

I make the comparison to a salesperson because that is what we all are in life. Whether we have worked in sales or not, we have to communicate effectively to achieve our goals. The good news is that we're selling the best product we know: ourselves!

Phone Call Script.

Using the headings, write down your notes and plans prior to making your phone call. Review the list carefully to ensure you are well prepared to address all issues.

☐ Minimum Goals

☐ Points to Stress Now

My Positive Qualities

My Experience

☐ Points to Save for Later

☐ Questions

If you don't believe you possess the necessary skills and that you are the best person for the job, how can you hope to be successful? The product you are selling is yourself. If you can overcome any self-doubt and you believe that you are right for a particular role, then the problem of phone phobia should start to fade.

As you go through life, you learn that if you don't paddle your own canoe, you don't move.

Katharine Hepburn (1907–),
Academy Award-winning
actress, writer

SUMMARY

Although talking to someone you have never spoken to before can be difficult, you must overcome your fear to achieve your goals. Making a successful call to initiate contact with a prospective employer is your first opportunity to impress.

The initial call is important. A successful telephone call starts the process of obtaining a face-to-face interview, and that's where you get the opportunity to sell yourself: in person rather than over the telephone.

• *Assessing your level of phone phobia.* By identifying your level of phone phobia honestly, you'll help yourself address the reasons for your discomfort and deal with the difficulties accordingly.

• *Reasons for phone phobia.* It is important to understand the common reasons for phone phobia and to identify which reason is most likely to interfere with your personal job prospecting.

• *What's the worst that can happen?* Face facts, and realize that the worst thing that can happen to you by making a call really isn't that terrible. There may be a number of different reasons for a cold response on the other end of the phone. Don't take rejection personally.

• *Remember friends and family.* Seek the help of friends and family who can help you establish contact with key targets. Often the people closest to us are the last ones we turn to for assistance. Yet they are most likely to be extremely willing to make an introductory phone call on your behalf.

• *Making a successful phone call.* Identify what you want to achieve, set your goals, and make the necessary preparations before you pick up the phone. What you say to yourself about prospecting has a powerful impact on how you perform when prospecting.

• *Pick up the phone.* Remember to remain positive and focus on the ultimate outcome you are striving for during the phone call. By thinking positively and visualizing the potential outcome of the call, you will start to convey a positive image to all those you communicate with.

CHAPTER 10

Successful Interviews and Meetings

Meeting a potential employer can be an unpleasant, or even a terrifying, experience if you're not adequately prepared. If you want to be truly successful, you'll probably need to pursue interviews confidently at various stages in your career. And if you hope to convince the interviewer that you're the best person for the job, you'll also have to perform well during the discussion.

Although this chapter focuses on the interview, the suggestions I offer can be applied to any sales meeting. In fact, an employment interview is a sales meeting, with a first-class product: you! It's a perfect example of a situation where you have the opportunity to use a limited, precious amount of time to present yourself directly to your target audience.

SET GOALS FOR YOUR INTERVIEW

I visited Amazon.com a moment ago and ran a search on the word *interview.* I was greeted with 1,023 matches, and I'll bet that number will have increased by the time I finish writing this sentence. The point is that there are endless books and articles on how to handle yourself in an interview. I certainly don't want to try to duplicate them. But I do want to offer a number of practical suggestions I've learned throughout my own career that have worked for me. For example, I believe that you should always write out a clear list of the questions you want to address in an interview, memorize them, ask them, and, finally, refer back to them after the meeting. Which questions worked? Which didn't?

Also, jotting down notes on the entire experience after an interview helps you in at least two ways. It will help you prepare for the next step, should you progress to the next interview phase. And it will help you fine-tune your message for meetings with other potential employers. If you continue to edit your script, reinforcing what "sells" and changing or replacing what doesn't, you'll develop a very clear style and line of questioning. That will help interviewers understand your skills clearly, assess your suitability for the role in question, and, most important, determine your potential future within the company.

It is also useful to develop a set of minimum goals and maximum goals prior to each interview or meeting. Take time to articulate your goals, write them down, and memorize them. Minimum goals could include:

The only limit to our realization of tomorrow will be our doubts of today.

Franklin D. Roosevelt
(1882–1945), thirty-second
president of the United States

- A referral to another two contacts
- An opportunity to meet another person in this organization
- The names of key competitors
- A commitment from the person you talk with for another meeting within the next month

Your maximum goals will be far more robust and might include:

- An assignment to complete a prototype case study to demonstrate your skills

- Active consideration for a role within the organization

- In addition to referrals, a commitment by your interviewer to contact those people on your behalf

- A job offer

You may be amazed by the progress you make toward achieving your goals if you simply set them out, write them down, and memorize your minimum and maximum objectives before each interview or meeting.

RESEARCH THE COMPANY

Let me tell you your worst interview nightmare. You work diligently to arrange an interview with a key decision maker at the company of your dreams, whose first question is, "So, what do you know about our company?"

You realize that you know nothing at all.

I have witnessed this nightmare in the unforgiving light of day. I've interviewed people for positions with DBM whose questions and comments made it clear that they knew absolutely nothing about our business. You can imagine how those interviews turned out.

A company's Web site is the first place to look for information about a potential employer. There you'll find:

- The annual report

- Financial statements and investor information

- Product and service information

- Recent press releases and announcements

- History and background of the company

- Office details (location and people)

- Career opportunities within the company

- Insights into the company's culture and style

Keep in mind, however, that the information a company posts on its Web site is the information it wants you to see. Also, the data are only as good as the person who created them and only as current as the most recent update. At many Web sites, even those of major companies, that may be not very recent at all. The point is that you'll need to do more research on a company than just look at a Web site. A company's site is an extremely useful tool, however, and it will give you clues on where else to look for further research.

Don't forget to contact people you know who have some association with the organization you're researching. This group could include customers, suppliers, and even competitors of the company, all of whom may have valuable insight into its culture and operations.

The salesman who sat up last night preparing today's call will not have to stay awake tonight worrying about what went wrong.

Author unknown

The amount of information available through research, on-line and otherwise, can be overwhelming. You can waste a great deal of time searching the Internet and then looking through newspapers, books, and other information sources. The trick is to do just enough research to reach the next stage of your job search.

In fact, many people prefer to analyze rather than act. Don't fall into the trap of analysis paralysis, continuing to do research while putting off a telephone call to set up a meeting. Be aware that some people tend to enjoy the research process of job search to the extent that they use it as an excuse for not doing much else. You cannot demonstrate your skills through research, unless, of course, you want a job as a researcher. Even then, you'll still have to have face-to-face meetings to secure the position.

So how much research is enough? A prospective employer doesn't expect you to have an intimate knowledge of the business. However, by conducting an adequate amount of research, you should be able to pursue a

Rewired, Rehired, or Retired?

position within an organization confidently if you are aware of the following information on it:

- The industry
- Its main competitors
- Its management structure
- Public information on it
- The goods or services it produces or sells
- A feeling of the culture
- Any recent headlines about it
- The outlook for the industry generally (is it growing or declining?)

BE KIND TO GATEKEEPERS

You need to speak to the right person to arrange a meeting or interview. This individual is likely to be incredibly busy and thus difficult to contact. As a result, you'll typically need to deal with a gatekeeper—a receptionist, personal assistant, secretary, assistant manager, divisional manager, public relations manager, human resource manager, or someone else whose role is to sift through phone calls, letters, faxes, and e-mails to protect that person from wasting valuable time.

In preparing for battle I have always found that plans are useless, but planning is indispensable.

Dwight D. Eisenhower (1890–1969), thirty-fourth president of the United States

This is not just a formality. Gatekeepers typically carry a lot of weight and influence in terms of who gets through to the people whose gates they guard. The more professional the gatekeeper is, the more difficult it may be to accomplish this, because part of that person's job description is usually to protect the time of the individual he or she works for. A phone call that sounds as if it might be a request for a favor or even a job may not register as a particularly high priority.

Here are a few tips for getting the cooperation of gatekeepers—or avoiding them completely by making direct contact with your target:

- *Call before 8:00 A.M., after 6:00 P.M., or between noon and 1:00 P.M.* (The exact times may vary depending on normal work patterns.) If you're lucky, the person you are calling will pick up the phone, or a fill-in receptionist will transfer your call without questioning you.
- *Give the gatekeeper options.* People tend to respond more positively when they're given options. You could say, "I'm trying to arrange a meeting with [name]. I'm available at 10:00 on Tuesday or 11:00 on Wednesday. Which time would be better?"
- *Always treat gatekeepers with respect.* Be polite. Never talk down to anyone. This needs no explanation in terms of simple civility, but there are practical issues at work here too. Following every recruiting interview I conduct, I ask Jane, my receptionist, and Lyn, my assistant, for their assessment of the candidate. Any applicant who fails to treat Jane and Lyn respectfully and professionally loses any chance of consideration. Their input is also vital to me in terms of whether a person will fit in well with our company. This is a simple yet effective approach to filtering people out. You should treat people equally, regardless of position.
- *Talk to the gatekeepers in the same tone as you would speak to their boss.* In other words, be open with them, and tell them directly what you want to discuss. There's no need for unnecessary small talk. These people are also extremely busy, so get to the point of your call, and always be polite, honest, and respectful.
- *Don't sell on the phone.* Remember that the goal of the call is to get someone interested in you, not to get a job offer. Once you obtain an interview over the phone, you can use your face-to-face meeting to sell your skills and experience. If you use up your ammunition during a phone call, you'll eliminate any reason for the person to want to see you in person.
- *Send an e-mail or fax instead of making a phone call.* Most people look at e-mails or faxes—perhaps not immediately but eventually. This is a great way to introduce yourself and highlight your strengths efficiently. Write that

you will call the following week to set up a brief meeting to cover what you have outlined in your e-mail. Mention that you're looking for only fifteen minutes of this very busy person's time.

THE VIRTUE—AND POTENTIAL VICE—OF PERSISTENCE

Persistence can be a virtue or a vice. It all depends on how you act. Learning how persistence can work to your advantage can be a valuable lesson. But understanding when to retreat is important too. There comes a time when continued pursuit is futile. You are the best judge of potential opportunities and of how long you should continue pushing them.

The people who get on in this world are the people who get up and look for the circumstances they want, and, if they can't find them, make them.

George Bernard Shaw (1856–1950), Irish-born British dramatist

Here are some tactics for following up with people without offending them:

• *Send a follow-up e-mail every few weeks.* This lets the person know you remain interested and provides news of what you're doing. Select a few key points that are likely to interest your contacts—for example:

"Since we met, I've focused my attention on the printing industry. Can you help by suggesting people I should be contacting? I'm trying to get a better understanding of the industry and identify opportunities that would suit my skills and abilities."

"In our meeting and in other meetings with other people, I've heard again and again that my prime skills are lifting the contributions of people within an organization and helping them develop their careers. This is certainly an area I enjoy, and I would appreciate any thoughts you may have to help me explore this interest further."

"After meeting with you and gaining a better understanding of your business, I believe I can make a contribution to your company in the area of systems development. Specifically, I have an idea for creating new policies and procedures that will have a significant impact on profitability."

• *Send an e-mail with a suggestion relevant to improving your contact's business.* Choose your words carefully to be sure you don't offend—for example:

"Clearly your operations and geographical reach have expanded dramatically in the past few years. I believe my skills from my previous role in centralized purchasing could assist you greatly. I can think of a number of ways to coordinate your purchasing to achieve the lowest cost and highest quality, identify the best service providers for your business, and, ultimately, improve your profitability."

[When dealing with the chief executive] "Recognizing the significant change that has occurred in your industry over the past two years, I believe my track record and experience in developing strategic plans could help you identify key areas of future opportunity."

"You mentioned that maintaining accurate monitoring of how your competitors are doing is a real challenge for your organization. May I suggest developing a competitive analysis by building a profile that identifies differences between your company and your competitors. I think it would help identify areas of relative strength to understand the competitive situation better. This may be a way to enhance your sales planning to lift sales and thus improve profitability."

Rewired, Rehired, or Retired?

- *Send your contact a copy of a relevant magazine, newspaper article, or Web page address.*
- *Send brief letters (no more than three paragraphs) on a regular basis— for example:*

> "I have given a lot of thought to our discussion and believe I can make a real contribution to your company. At no cost to you, I'm prepared to spend one month working with you to prove my value. During that time, I think you'll see the contributions I can make. I'm fully prepared to perform or perish based on what I achieve."

This approach may seem dramatic, but it demonstrates your level of commitment and interest in the organization and can be extremely effective. If you prove your worth, you'll have removed much of the risk that always exists for companies when they hire new people. After all, there is very little downside for the company. At the very least, the people you are talking with will sit up and take notice. If you are unemployed at the time, the worst that can happen is that you will gain further experience in that particular industry. What have you got to lose?

- *Make a follow-up phone call every two months.* Mention that you would just like to talk to the person for *two minutes* to give him or her a brief update of your situation. Make sure you stick to your two-minute limit for your side of the communication. Show that you know how to get to the point. The conversation could lead to an invitation for a meeting.

In my own experience as a consultant working with companies on strategic planning and restructuring, I have found that this persistent approach often works. I've learned afterward that a company retained me precisely because they were impressed with my persistence and with the fact that I didn't offend people or overstay my welcome in the process. My persistence in focusing on their issues strongly showed that I cared about their business and would take the same approach when I worked for them.

Never think that making contact is a one-off process. Don't assume that people will call you back. It is up to you to take things further and initiate next steps.

Case Study: Take the Initiative and Make the Call

When I started my own consulting business after working in the banking industry for more than two decades, it became clear from the start that my customers (or, to be more precise, my potential customers) were very busy people. I often joked that my company didn't need to be in the telephone directory during the first seven years of the business: no one was going to look up my number to call me back. And, in fact, although I'm sure that most people had the best intentions to return my calls, they usually didn't. I always followed up as a result, phoning back two to four weeks after my first attempt.

By taking an active approach and continuing to follow up on a regular basis when I believed there was potential for a job, the initiative was always with me. I was not sitting by the telephone in the vain hope that someone might just return my calls. This helped me build the business very quickly.

It may help to visualize yourself as the person you are trying to approach. Consider how he or she may think and feel, and then act accordingly. If a woman approaching you for a sales job possessed certain skills that you were interested in and if she were persistent in a positive way, wouldn't her interest interest you? If she works so hard to sell her skills and experience to you, isn't it likely that she would show the same enthusiasm with your customers? Wouldn't you want to find out?

THE FACE-TO-FACE MEETING

No matter how well you write a resumé and cover letter, the key is to get in the door for an all-important face-to-face interview. This is where a potential employer or client gets to know you and your capabilities.

Rewired, Rehired, or Retired?

In the past, the primary focus of an interview tended to be the candidate's qualifications and experience. If they were suitable for the position, the individual was likely to get the job. It's no longer that simple, and rightly so. Assessing a person's suitability for a role is often done by considering the individual from three perspectives that are often referred to as "can do," "will do," and "best fit."

Be yourself. Who else is better qualified?

Frank J. Giblin II

• *Can do.* This relates to qualifications and experience. Is it clear that you can do the job? Do your academic credentials and past employment experience demonstrate that you have the attributes needed to do the job confidently? In the past, many employers relied solely on "can do" to make their decisions.

• *Will do.* This is a question of fire in the belly—that is, your perceived motivation to be successful in a specific role. I've met thirty year olds who demonstrate the energy (or lack of energy) of an eighty year old and many fifty year olds whose energy levels would make you think they were thirty. So it's not entirely a physical issue (although you'd be amazed how physical fitness sends out powerful "will do" signals). You demonstrate "will do" in an interview by making the distinct impression that you are determined to succeed and contribute to the success of the company.

• *Best fit.* This is a function of how well an individual will fit into an organization's culture. It is reflected in many factors, including personality, appearance, and personal preferences. Although they are difficult to quantify, it is absolutely essential that you demonstrate good fit characteristics. The interview is usually the only place where interviewers can get a good sense of fit.

If you make it onto the short list for a job, it is usually understood that you possess the right qualifications for the position. Making a difference at this point in the selection process often comes down to how well you handle the "will do" and "best fit" aspects of a final interview.

Don't be fooled by the fact that because you possess the relevant skills and can confidently handle a telephone conversation, you will get the job. Many interviews fail as a result of personality clashes, not because of lack of skill. There is no substitute for the face-to-face interview to allow you to truly shine.

Always be yourself, and tell the truth during an interview. Don't try to be someone you're not. Don't act in a particular way or stretch the truth about your skills just to fit in with an interviewer's line of questioning.

Case Study: Be Honest About Your Skills

On being approached by a major women's retail fashion chain to gauge my interest in becoming a director of the company, I was asked about my experience in the retail industry and women's fashion in particular. I told them that ladies' fashion was something I knew very little about, that shopping was not one of my favorite pastimes, and that I probably spent less than two hours a year at it.

My response was unexpected but, it turned out, exactly the right thing to say. Because the other directors had years of experience in the industry, the company was seeking a new director with strategic and business management skills, plus an ability to assist in financial analysis. The other directors were emotionally involved in the industry. I was not. And my skills were ideal for the position. It was clear that I would never get carried away by the glamour and emotion of the industry.

By being completely honest, I demonstrated how I was different from other people being considered for the role. I subsequently built a great relationship with the company and joined the board as the chairman.

THE 10/50 RULE: LESS IS MORE

Here is a single rule of thumb that will improve your effectiveness significantly in any meeting you attend: for every hour of a meeting, try to talk for no more than ten minutes and listen for the other fifty (this is known as the 10/50 rule). This may seem radical in an interview setting—where the whole idea is to sell yourself and your skills—but think about it. You may end up talking for more than ten minutes, but perhaps your initial goal could be to talk for no more than thirty minutes. The more practice you have at controlling the amount of talk in an interview, the more skillful you will become at asking probing questions.

You may believe that you should talk as much as possible in an interview, trying to squeeze in as many positives about yourself as you can during your allotted time. Of course, you need to sell yourself, but do it thoughtfully, and prepare carefully.

No one has a finer command of language than the person who keeps his mouth shut.

Sam Rayburn (1882–1961), U.S. congressman and Speaker of the House of Representatives

Most interviewers have a range of questions they'll need to ask to assess your suitability for the position. Although it's your big chance to prove yourself, you'll need to respect the interviewer's time frame. (Remember the I-SPEAK communication styles and listening techniques discussed in Chapter Six.)

In this environment, you're likely to help your cause more by proving you have researched the company and displaying your interest and intelligence than by talking about how wonderful you are. Asking the right questions helps you set a positive imprint in the interviewer's mind—for example:

"You have established a new factory at [location]. What have been your main challenges in the first few months?"

"You have been losing market share in two key areas. What strategies do you plan to implement to reverse the situation?"

"How have you been able to handle cultural differences when you brought the two companies together in the recent merger?"

"What are the succession plans when your current CEO retires?"

"What is the long-term outlook for the *X* division, considering new competitive and technological advancements?"

Questions like these show that you've done your homework. Asking them also helps you probe the interviewer and get beyond a superficial view of the company.

Most people enjoy talking about themselves and their business. If you ask a few key questions, the interviewer may provide you with a wealth of information about the company and the position. The information will help you gauge your interest in the position. Remember that getting a job is a two-way street. You want the *right* job, not just any job.

Having the discipline to try not to talk more than ten minutes in an hour is a worthwhile goal to focus on to achieve success. Granted, it isn't always easy, particularly at the start. It might be beneficial to practice this skill by recording an interview with a friend or keeping it in mind in any group setting. It certainly goes against the expectations of most interviewers, and in that sense, it will help you stand out from the crowd.

The real art of conversation is not only to say the right thing in the right place, but to leave unsaid the wrong thing at the tempting moment.

Lady Dorothy Nevill (1826–1913), society hostess, horticulturist

DECISION INFLUENCERS AND DECISION MAKERS

Many of us tend to spend an enormous amount of time trying to identify, focus on, and ultimately impress perceived decision makers. In the process, we may neglect an equally important group, the decision influencers, that is, people who are likely to contribute to any final decision the decision maker reaches. One obvious example is the situation in which, having made it onto the short list for a job, you're asked to meet two or three other executives before a final decision is made. They probably won't get you the job, but they may very well be in a position to deny it to you.

We usually think we know who the key decision maker is, but even then it may be a guess. Some people might act low key; others might act in an authoritarian manner, giving the impression they are in charge.

Rewired, Rehired, or Retired?

I have been surprised more than once in the past in a selling situation where I have believed a person was the decision maker, only to find that the person was posturing (and obviously trying to score a free lunch). On further probing and asking independent questions, I discovered the real decision maker was someone else, although the person I had been dealing with was a decision influencer.

Treat Everyone with Equal Respect

Not all decision influencers are so easily identified. This suggests a simple, foolproof rule: treat everyone, no matter how insignificant anyone may appear, with exactly the same respect you would reserve for the prime decision maker. This should not only apply to business situations, of course, but to every other area of your life as well. Showing respect ought to come naturally. People who are fake and insincere toward others are usually caught in the end. Don't modify your behavior to be someone other than your natural self because that will get you nowhere. Be particularly sensitive to this in the business environment. You're certainly trying to show a group of people your skills and abilities, but you also need to demonstrate the ease with which you'd be able to become part of their team.

People Associated with the Organization

Another important category of decision influencers includes people who are not employed by the company you are seeking to work with but are known to and respected by its leaders. Do you know—or can you arrange an introduction to—someone who is a client, supplier, or friend to key people in the organization? A telephone call by such an individual to a key decision maker can carry an enormous amount of weight as an independent view or source of information. At the very least, it is likely to move you to the top of the list for an interview.

Retired Business Executives

Retired business executives are valuable but often neglected decision influencers. You may assume that because this individual is no longer active in the day-to-day operations of the company, he or she is no longer important or effective. As I noted previously, there is a lingering stereotype that retired people are no longer capable of sharp thinking and have lost their touch with the real business world. This is far from the truth, particularly with many retired businesspeople I know. They keenly observe changes and trends in the business world and keep their contacts warm. Finally, precisely because they have removed themselves from the day-to-day pressures of business, people who have retired are likely to have the time and the interest to assist you.

One of the most powerful decision influencers I have ever known is my previous chairman, who is now seventy-nine years old. He has retired from all executive responsibilities and director's commitments, but he is still extremely active. He maintains many business interests and continues to act as a rainmaker for his old company, generating new business for the firm. Because he has stayed fresh and maintained contact with key people, and is widely admired and highly respected, a word from him can open most doors in the business world. Think about the people you know from all walks of life who might fill such a role for you.

IS IT THE RIGHT JOB FOR YOU?

Identifying the right next step in your career is vital to achieving the greater goal of happiness and self-fulfillment. Many people lose focus of their real needs when it comes to job seeking. As some of us have learned from experience, poverty is surely a great motivator. Most of us must be employed if we intend to pay our mortgage or rent and support a family if we have one. But even in that situation, taking the time to look at exactly what job we would like, and in what environment we would ideally prefer to work, empowers us to achieve our goals faster.

As you pursue a job opportunity, don't relinquish control of your destiny. Be wary of the interviewer who spends an entire interview selling the position and the company to you, for example, never asking relevant questions about your interests and experience. Your interest in a particular position can be magnified by the enthusiasm of your potential employer. You may have been identified as ideally suited for the position, or even better than anyone had hoped for! It's your responsibility to determine that once you land the job, it will still be the right position for you.

Starting a new job, only to find it is less than what you anticipated, is a terrible experience that can cause enormous stress, frustration, and disappointment. Be honest with yourself. Don't be fooled by a flashy office or a fast-talking recruiter. Get to the soul of the company. Ask questions. Financial pressures may hinder your ability to attain utopia, but at the very least, assure yourself that you know what you're getting into.

Case Study: Get to the Soul of a Prospective Employer

Early in my career, I was the manager of a bank branch and had established a very strong business relationship with a local manufacturing company. I must have impressed them, as they asked me to leave the bank and become their chief executive, even though I knew very little about their industry.

Given my modest income at the time, I was naturally excited by the prospects that this new position could provide: a better standard of living for my family, a nicer company car, and so forth.

Perhaps it was my conservative banking background that made me decide on a safe option. I suggested to my potential employer that I take a week's annual leave from the bank to work with the new company for free. At the end of that week, I would make my decision about joining the company.

Four hours into the first day, I knew the arrangement wasn't for me, as I became aware of elements of the business that I would never have seen from the outside. By the end of the first day, I realized that continuing in the bank was far and away my better option.

This simple step saved me an enormous amount of time and disruption to my career. The experience taught me a great lesson: it's only when you work inside an organization that you really get to know it.

SUMMARY

Performing well in an interview puts you in a position of power. Not only does the exercise provide valuable experience for the future, but it also gives you the confidence and ability to choose whether a position offered suits your needs and goals.

Remember these points:

• *Set goals for your interview.* Identify beforehand what you want to achieve. Write down the questions you want to ask the interviewer. Following the interview, review your questions, and jot down notes from the interview for future reference. Articulate minimum and maximum goals before every interview.

• *Research the company.* Do your homework by researching the company prior to an interview. You can find a wealth of information on a company's Web site and in newspapers, business magazines, and books. Contact everyone and anyone you know who may be familiar with the organization.

• *Be kind to gatekeepers.* Understand the role of individuals who filter information to the person you are pursuing. Treat them with respect. Be creative in your efforts to arrange an interview. Be careful not to provide too much information over the phone so that you don't reduce the level of interest in meeting you in person.

• *The virtue—and potential vice—of persistence.* If you think there is an opportunity within an organization, maintain regular contact in a way that won't offend or make you appear pushy. Ongoing contact reminds decision makers of your situation and your continued interest in the company. Persistence conducted in a nonoffensive manner is impressive.

• *The face-to-face meeting.* Remember that meeting an interviewer in person presents your best opportunity to shine, demonstrating your skills and suitability for a position. Be yourself. Let your personality come through to help the employer assess whether you will be a suitable fit in the organization. Remember that "can do," "will do," and "best fit" are all necessary to be a winner.

• *The 10/50 rule: Less is more.* Communicate clearly and effectively in an interview, choosing your words with care. Let the interviewer do most of the talking. Listen carefully to what is said. Make it clear that you have conducted your own research into the company to demonstrate your serious interest in the position.

• *Decision influencers and decision makers.* Be aware of the people responsible for both influencing and making the decision about whether to hire you. Often someone who is well respected by the company, such as a retired executive, will be happy to pass on a recommendation for you.

• *Is it the right job for you?* Maintain your focus on what you want to achieve from the interview. Identify whether a job is right for you, even if the interviewer is enthusiastic about employing you. Don't be afraid to ask questions in the interview, and be honest with yourself about your own career goals.

CHAPTER 11

Global Opportunities for the Mature Worker

A society for all ages is multigenerational. It is not fragmented, with youths, adults and older persons going their separate ways. Rather it is age-inclusive with different generations recognizing—and acting upon—their commonality of interest.
Kofi Annan (1938–), United Nations secretary general, when launching the International Year of Older Persons

The globalization of corporations has created further opportunities to work from different countries (thanks largely to the Internet explosion). There are more choices for us to work where we want to. This means that many of us may contemplate living in a country other than our home country and perhaps even retire there.

This chapter contains observations from around the globe of retirement practices, government intervention, influences, and assistance provided to mature workers. As you will see, we live in a world where practices, support, and attitudes toward mature workers differ markedly. By looking at what is currently happening around the world, we can see how retired and mature workers fit into the various working environments and the encouragement and support given to them by their government.

Now that we have plunged headlong into the twenty-first century, attitudes and expectations toward older workers are gradually aligning with the reality of extended life expectancy and an improved quality of life for older workers. In most countries throughout the world today, there is a trend to eliminate discrimination against older workers and to design more suitable employment conditions. Governments around the globe have been forced to shift their attitudes and provide better solutions for their aging population.

The decision to make age sixty-five the marker of retirement and old age is a historical oddity: it was a "line in the sand" decision made by Chancellor Otto von Bismarck as Germany designed an old-age pension plan. Age sixty-five was identified as the time for retirement and the indicator of old age over a century ago by a Prussian general, when average life expectancy was actually much less than sixty-five.

In some cultures, the normal retirement age is different: it is fifty-five in Korea, for example, and sixty in Japan. In Australia and New Zealand, a mandatory retirement age has been eliminated on the basis of antidiscrimination.

> The Swedish government recently instituted a program allowing workers to retire up to four years before or three years after the normal pensionable age of sixty-seven, with an actuarial adjustment of 0.6 percent more or less pension money for each month of deviation from the normal retirement age. Similarly, Canada now lets older workers determine their own retirement age by providing an adjustment of .5 percent per month of deviation up or down from their usual pensionable age of sixty-five.
>
> Other European countries are examining the possibilities of a "retirement decade"—a period initially between the ages of sixty and seventy—during which individuals, with full knowledge of the economic consequences, may choose their own retirement age. It is hoped that this flexible approach will allow more workers to work longer if they wish.*
>
> Ken Dychtwald, *Age Power* (1999).

*From AGE POWER by Ken Dychtwald, copyright © 1999 by Ken Dychtwald, Ph.D. Used by permission of Jeremy P. Tarcher, a division of Penguin Putnam, Inc.

In the United States, retirement and age sixty-five remain virtually synonymous. This misperception, however, is beginning to change. The Social Security "normal" retirement age (i.e., for full benefits) for anyone younger than forty-one is now sixty-seven. Moreover, Congress has protected workers from age discrimination beginning at age forty. Phased retirement can begin as early as age fifty. Those who have worked at a job for twenty-five or thirty years may be eligible for retirement at forty-five or fifty. And the most common age at which Americans actually begin to receive Social Security is sixty-two.

AARP, Beyond 50—A Report to the Nation on Economic Security, May 2001.

Tinkering with official retirement dates, however, may well be an inadequate response to the challenge ahead. Each year, for example, over 4 million men and women will join the ranks of those over age fifty in the United States.

In the year 2000, approximately 76 million Americans were over the age of fifty, the total number of the entire American population in 1900.[*]

Ken Dychtwald, *Age Power* (1999).

Regrettably, pension plans throughout the world have inadequately prepared for the aging population and are ill equipped to provide enough support to those in their later years. We're living longer, so our demands will continue to put pressure on governments to readdress pension plans and existing retirement ages. Because of this lack of planning, particularly in some European countries, the working population is funding retirees through very large mandatory retirement contributions.

SUPPORT FOR MATURE WORKERS

In most countries, social security or a pension is paid by the government to older people without a regular income to assist with the expenses of daily living. Usually this amount is based on the individual's salary base and contributions made to a fund over a period of time.

[*]From AGE POWER by Ken Dychtwald, copyright © 1999 by Ken Dychtwald, Ph.D. Used by permission of Jeremy P. Tarcher, a division of Penguin Putnam, Inc.

Another major direction of pension reform is toward private management and compulsory savings schemes. Chile has recently been the developing-country model for pension privatization and other Latin American nations have adopted aspects of the Chilean system. Variations on the privatization theme are likewise being instituted in parts of Eastern Europe and the former Soviet Union as these nations make the transition from command to market economies. Even in Europe and North America, where pension systems arguably have been most successful, there is mounting pressure to shift the emphasis more clearly toward private and compulsory arrangements.

Loraine A. West and Kevin Kinsella, "Pension Management and Reform in Asia: An Overview," *NBR Exectuive Insight, 11,* May 1997. Seattle, WA: The National Bureau of Asian Research.

Many of us take for granted that our government will offer some support for people in retirement. There are, however, some countries (Thailand, for example) in which the government provides little or no assistance to older workers, because the assumption is that families take care of these individuals in their later years.

Until recently, the government in Hong Kong provided pension benefits only to civil servants; there was no regulation that companies should provide any retirement benefits. In 2000, a new scheme was introduced to help other members of the workforce save for their own retirement.

In the United Kingdom, baby boomers with long working histories in a top company or the civil service typically benefit from a generous pension deal. Firms such as ICI, Shell, BP, and Marks & Spencer have traditionally treated their employees well, offering final salary packages that pay a pension relative to earnings at retirement. Regrettably, these packages are not always offered to employees. People in the United Kingdom are becoming better at planning for their own retirement by boosting pension investment through allocating part of their salary entitlement and taking out personal pension plans.

Whether the government in your country provides benefits or not, one message comes through loud and clear: we must all ensure our futures with the help of planned savings or continued work, whether part time or full time.

Rewired, Rehired, or Retired?

As many more people move from their home country to live, work, and possibly retire in other countries, it is important to realize that these benefits differ widely across the world.

EARLY AND VOLUNTARY RETIREMENT PLANS

At the same time as improved health and changing ideas allow many people to work far longer than in the past, early or voluntary retirement plans are growing even more commonplace. Such plans are usually developed in response to restructurings or mergers and acquisitions. Employees may be offered a "golden parachute" to retire, and that may give their employers a legal way to thin their ranks of older workers.

In the United States, early retirement at the age of fifty-five has gained popularity over the past thirty years. American workers are better educated, have higher paid employment histories, and a higher average income than their parents' generation, so many can afford an earlier retirement. But at the same time, life expectancy has risen over the past thirty years, suggesting that early retirees will need to manage retirement income wisely and perhaps augment that income with part-time work.

In countries such as Hong Kong, Peru, Chile, Finland, and Japan, early retirement plans are usually offered only to top management or those in larger organizations.

UNDERSTANDING THE WORTH OF OLDER WORKERS

While golden parachutes and voluntary retirement plans are growing in popularity, at the same time there is an increasing awareness and appreciation of the continued worth of older workers. More governments and companies throughout the world are offering incentives for them to remain in the workforce.

In the United States, companies like PriceWaterhouseCoopers are attempting to entice workers over the age of fifty to stay on, offering three- and four-day workweeks, as well as telecommuting options, to valued older employees. The U.S. government has lifted restrictions, such as salary caps to social security recipients, so they can remain working without penalty.

In Canada, many organizations bring back retired employees on a consulting basis, paying them contractually for their services, even though they may have taken a voluntary retirement separation package. The government's Human Resource Development Division has started a program to assist the transition of older workers back into the workplace.

In Australia, some companies, recognizing the loss of experience when mature-age executives and managers elect to retire early, are offering part-time employment to executives who wish to expand lifestyle options.

Some nonprofit organizations have been set up in Belgium with a view to using valuable experienced workers to provide assistance to young companies at low cost. Mature workers are also often invited to use their talents and experience to coach younger managers in these companies.

The Japanese have a practice of finding less demanding job opportunities for senior executives as they reach their later careers. The government provides subsidies to companies that employ older workers and is also requesting that companies provide reemployment support for those who have retired.

In France, it costs employers more to terminate employees above age fifty than younger workers. The result is that companies are encouraged to retain older workers.

ATTITUDES TOWARD OLDER WORKERS

Even as companies and governments work to keep older employees in the workforce, many individuals find they are still discriminated against in the workplace, despite the introduction of laws prohibiting such behavior. In this fast-moving era of technical development, older workers can often be prejudicially considered behind the times simply on the basis of age.

Although younger workers usually respect the experience of older peers, they sometimes doubt their ability to be innovative or move quickly. Younger workers may also resent the "know-it-all" attitude of some older workers and question their reluctance to reach decisions quickly.

In Peru, people over the age of fifty outside the world of work are generally treated with respect. However, on occasion, elderly people have been openly discriminated against in obtaining jobs. Job advertisements in Peruvian newspapers have openly asked for "persons not older than . . ." despite a recently introduced law that prohibits any type of discrimination based on age, sex, religion, race, or social condition.

Traditionally, older people in Thailand are respected for cultural reasons and older workers are tolerated in the work environment if they are mentors or teachers. Culturally, older people still view status and power as a privilege, not a responsibility, whereas younger people are starting to see it the other way around.

In Korea, although mature workers are usually highly regarded, they are often perceived as not being flexible enough to deal with the current rate of change in that country.

The British government, after receiving a European Union (EU) directive, has recently signed a historic commitment to ban discrimination at work. Legislation to outlaw age discrimination has seemed likely for a while. The 1997 Treaty of Amsterdam extended EU regulations in equal opportunities to include age. A report on older workers from the Cabinet Office's Performance and Innovation Unit said that "age discrimination legislation would have a positive effect on British culture" (Cabinet Office, 2000).

TAKING ON FULL- OR PART-TIME ROLES

Many retired workers who accepted early retirement have now realized that the money they saved for retirement will not last for their lifetime. Therefore, many are returning or looking to return to the workplace. Aside from economic and longevity factors, there is the life interest issue. Many retirees do not look with relish to thirty years of leisure and require what they consider to be meaningful engagement to maintain lifestyle balance.

Part-time work and project and volunteer assignments have appeal to retirees. Recent legislation in the United States has provided incentives to older workers to return to the workplace. Since the year 2000, this legislation has raised the amount that retirees can earn while still drawing full social security payments.

To highlight the differences between nations and their government's response to the issue of aged workers, in Peru there are limited incentives for people of a mature age to continue working at all. This is largely due to the fact that 40 percent of the population (10.6 million people) is now nineteen years old or younger, meaning that the demand for jobs for young people is squeezing out opportunities for mature workers.

Due largely to the fact that so many older workers have been prepensioned, there is now a growing trend around the world to entice mature workers back into the workplace because of their experience and knowledge. In Chile, there is now a trend to employ more mature workers as independent consultants in organizations, particularly in family enterprises where more outsiders are being employed for their executive experience. Similarly, mature workers in Korea are taking on more roles as business turnaround consultants for problematic companies on a part-time or contractual basis.

Tom Griffiths retired as a telephone repairman at the end of his shift at the New York Stock Exchange one Friday last fall [2000], "just as if I was going home to put my feet up on the porch," he said. Come Monday morning, though, he was back on the trading floor, fixing the same telephone lines, this time as a part-time worker, with his pension making up for the lost income.

"I was a little leery" of accepting the offer to "sort of" retire, admitted Mr. Griffiths, a 52-year-old Staten Island resident. But his employer offered cash bonuses to encourage older workers to exchange their job security and full-time compensation for a novel blend of work and retirement.

"I had a lot of bills," Mr. Griffiths said. "That was the driving force for me to take it." His incentives included $10,000, two years' salary and the chance to win future bonuses. . . .

A number of large companies, including Avaya, Monsanto, PepsiCo and Lockheed Martin, are now finding ways to work around the legal obstacles and offer phased retirement.

Phased retirement can take many forms. At universities, it is used to clear out elderly tenured professors. But in the private sector, it is being promoted as a way to keep valued older workers in a tight labor market. Workers in their 50s who would otherwise take advantage of early retirement provisions in their pensions are offered the chance to work reduced hours and supplement their reduced incomes by tapping those pensions.

Other analysts wonder whether phased retirement is not just a new way of turning America's veteran employees into contingent workers, allowing corporations to subsidize their compensation costs by drawing down surplus pension assets.

"These are highly skilled, functional people, and they're being converted into part-time workers," said David C. Howard, a St. Louis lawyer who has represented former Monsanto workers in age-discrimination suits. "There's a whole across-the-board range of benefits that they're being excluded from. They're not getting merit-pay increases, advancements, promotions."

At Avaya, Michael A. Dennis, a vice president who negotiated his company's program, argued that phased retirement is a tool for preserving good jobs with benefits. . . .

Employees in their mid-50s tend to present big liabilities, pension accruals, wages buoyed by seniority, rising health care costs. For those reasons, it was popular in the 1980s and 1990s to urge costly 55-year-olds to the door. Even after paying them cash incentives to retire, companies could replace them at lower cost with younger workers.

Now, though, after a decade of economic expansion, many companies find it hard to find skilled employees. Compensation consultants say retaining older employees is becoming more attractive, particularly as America's 76 million baby boomers age. The oldest boomers are turning 55 this year, an age at which most big companies with traditional pensions offer early retirement.

Worse, it has become apparent that when early retirees leave, they often take new jobs at other companies. And then they no longer look so expensive; many will work for wages only, because they already have health insurance and pensions.

Avaya's Mr. Dennis said this was on his mind as he drafted the company's phased-retirement plan. "We didn't want these folks retiring and going around and working for other companies that would be competing against us," he said. The breakthrough, he said, was finding a legal way of giving the older workers their pensions and keeping them in-house.

Other companies are offering similar arrangements on a smaller scale, said Anna Rappaport, who surveyed 232 private and public-sector employers for the William M. Mercer consulting firm.

She found that 36 percent were hiring back retirees as consultants and independent contractors without benefits, and 37 percent were hiring them back for part-time and temporary assignments.

Mary Williams Walsh, "No Time to Put Your Feet Up as Retirement Comes in Stages," New York Times, April 15, 2001.*

In Canada, DBM has been assisting individuals from fifty-five to sixty-four years of age make the transition back into the workforce. One individual was appointed chief mentoring officer for a medium-sized dot-com company. These individuals have been specifically chosen for their "gray hair"; the organizations were looking for business skills rather than technical skills.

Many organizations employ older workers of retirement age to work on special projects such as strategic planning, sales, and finance. Some nonprofit organizations have been set up to use experienced workers to help young companies at low cost and to coach younger managers in these companies. Older workers are especially appreciated in the service or hospitality industries and in human resources, and general management.

Older workers in Hong Kong often find they are not prepared for the change of pace when they reach retirement age. At the age of sixty-five, 52.5 percent of all women and 13.6 percent of all men live alone, and the loss of workplace and social contacts creates a significant void in their lives. Often, they choose to take on part-time positions or consultant assignments to help fill this void.

An example of an older worker successfully taking on a part-time role was demonstrated recently by a participant in the DBM outplacement pro-

Rewired, Rehired, or Retired?

gram in Peru. After holding the position of general manager of a bottling company, this man has now turned his hand to being a consultant-coach-trainer at a local courier company. He is receiving a higher yearly income by teaching a young general manager the secrets of managing.

In Australia, more and more opportunities are now provided for senior executives to focus on part-time roles and consulting. Recently, an executive director of one of the largest banks in Australia wished to take retirement and was given the opportunity to change his work and lifestyle. He now works three days a week at the bank, and the other two days he dedicates to his role as chairman of a performing arts group. Another example is of a former human resource director of one of the large mining companies who now runs a farm four days a week and works as a consultant for the other three days.

DEMOGRAPHIC TRENDS

In the United States, the vacuum caused by early-retiring baby boomers is affecting the workforce. The brain drain they are causing is of great concern to employers. This is especially true in the current economic downturn caused by the business failures of the high-technology sector where younger workers were the prized employees. Now the employer is seeing value in seasoned executives with years of experience and scar tissue. The over-fifty worker is now missed for these qualities and will be much sought after to return to the workplace, and on his or her own terms.

Rapidly aging populations as well as declining birthrates are also becoming big influences. For example, in Japan, as of 2000, 36 percent (23.9 million) of the overall working population of 65 million are aged fifty and over. This figure is forecast to rise to 38 percent in 2005 and 40 percent in 2010.

As Canada experiences a dramatic demographic shift—an aging population and a lack of young new talent—organizations are rediscovering the value of older workers to provide experience and maturity and are offering more flexible forms of employment. Recent statistics show that the working population of age fifty and over has increased by 9 percent since 1996 (Statistics Canada, 2001). This trend has opened up new opportunities for older workers seeking alternative forms of employment.

Similarly, the population of employees between the ages of forty and fifty-four in France increased from 30 percent in 1992 to 40 percent in 1999 (Insec, 2000). If workers over age fifty don't adapt to the new global economy, they're out. There is demand for those who do adapt due to their experience, but they are threatened by overwork, loss of balance, and burnout.

In Australia, more than 80 percent of the projected growth in the labor force between 1998 and 2016 will be in the group aged forty-five and up.

Interestingly, in Hong Kong, the number of workers over age fifty who obtained residency or citizenship in other countries prior to the 1997 handover will be tempted to relocate to those countries for their retirement years due to the high cost of living in Hong Kong. And younger professional workers who migrated to other countries prior to the handover are now returning to Hong Kong and competing with older workers for the same positions.

Finland has a shortage in the high-tech and Internet areas. There are very few foreigners in Finland, and many young Finns are studying abroad and may not return. Older people are following the taxation development whereby taxes should be lowered due to the EU, which they hope will keep more Finns in their native country.

Although the older population is projected to increase in most countries around the world, these trends fall into insignificance when compared to the tragic circumstances in South Africa. The advent of AIDS, which is most prevalent in the economically active sector of South Africa, could decimate the workforce by more than 25 percent over the next decade (South African Government Statistical Services, 2001). The working population in South Africa has been further hindered by an increase in emigration.

With 22 percent of its population aged 60 or older, Japan is currently the "oldest" of all Asian nations and demographically one of the oldest countries in the world. (Italy stands as the world's most aged major country with 23 percent of its populace aged 60 and over.) In contrast, fewer than 6 percent of all persons in the Philippines are among the ranks of the elderly. . . .

China alone will see its 60 and over population explode from 123 million in 1998 to nearly 280 million by the year 2025. . . .

Rewired, Rehired, or Retired?

By 2025, one of every three Japanese will be at least 60 years old, and the percentage of elderly will approach or exceed 25 percent in Hong Kong, Singapore, South Korea, and Taiwan. What sets many East and Southeast Asian nations apart from the developed countries of Europe and North America is the speed of the demographic aging process. Population aging in the latter has been a gradual process that allowed societies and economies time to adapt to their demographic evolution. For instance, it took 89 years for the elderly (60+) share of the total population to rise from 10 percent to 20 percent in Sweden. This same increase will be compressed into fewer than 30 years in most Asian economies, which suggests that Asian nations may not have the luxury of trial and error in terms of social program design. Fortunately for most economies in Asia, the increase in the percentage of elderly is expected to be relatively modest during the next decade, and then accelerate after the year 2010 as the large cohorts of persons born after World War II enter the ranks of the elderly. Thus, countries throughout the region have a window of opportunity, albeit a rapidly-closing one, to plan for the demographic aging of their populations.

Loraine A. West and Kevin Kinsella, "Pension Management and Reform in Asia: An Overview," NBR Exectuive Insight, 11, May 1997. Seattle, WA: The National Bureau of Asian Research.

THE EFFECT OF EXTENDED LIFE EXPECTANCY

U.S. census trends indicate that the total population of those age fifty and over was 75.9 million in 2001 and will grow to 87.4 million in 2006. The fastest-growing group in the United States is the number of people living to an age of between eighty and one hundred years (U. S. Bureau of Labor Statistics, 2001).

According to the same source, the fastest-growing segment of the workforce between 1996 and 2006 will be those aged fifty-five to sixty-four and they project that the median age of the labor force in 2008 will be 40.7 years.

Even those who have planned carefully for retirement are concerned about outliving their savings and becoming a burden to their children. Because of this, there is a trend for retirees to return to work to augment their retirement benefits and involve themselves with meaningful activity. Rather than retire in poverty, many mature workers are deciding to continue to work either full time or part time until they can afford to retire comfortably. They are also preferring to continue working to eliminate the possibility of becoming bored with retirement.

According to the AARP's "Beyond 50 Report" (2001), partly due to longer life expectancy, Americans age sixty-two to seventy-four are just warming up as far as retirement goes. Many in this generation do not envision sitting out their retirement on a three-legged stool but expect to be active, engaged, and working either full- or part-time. Today, more than thirty-two million Americans age fifty and older are in the workforce, and the number is rising.

In Japan, it is inevitable that older workers will constitute more of the labor market. With regard to thinking about individual careers, a paradigm shift is necessary, and people must realize that the world where once your position and how you were treated were proportionate to the number of years you worked is changing. Until now, the seniority system has been dominant; however, if the number of highly paid employees continues to increase, companies won't be able to operate. The current wage system is being reevaluated, and the Japanese are enduring unprecedented levels of layoffs in the workforce.

In the United Kingdom, baby boomers will be wealthier than their parents when they retire but are more likely to be unmarried and childless. Life expectancy is increasing by almost one year every three years, and there are now 1 million fewer people in their twenties than ten years ago. As the baby boomers retire, the numbers entering the workforce at the other end are shrinking progressively, a situation that ultimately will lead to a significant skills shortage.

Most of the world's older (60 and over) population now lives in developing countries, and within three decades, these nations will be home to 74 percent of the world's elderly. Population aging will

Rewired, Rehired, or Retired?

place a strain on the economies of all countries because of the growing need for retirement benefits and the higher costs of elderly health care. Developing countries also are finding that informal old-age support systems, such as family and mutual aid societies, which are often the mainstay of their social security system, tend to weaken and lose their traditional effectiveness as development and urbanization advance.

> Loraine A. West and Kevin Kinsella, "Pension Management and Reform in Asia: An Overview," *NBR Executive Insight, 11,* May 1997. Seattle, WA: The National Bureau of Asian Research.

There is currently a strong trend in many countries around the world to extend the retirement age to cure the pressure from the aging baby boomer employees to work longer. Because baby boomers did not have as many children as their parents (due in part to the zero population movement in the 1960s and 1970s), there are now fewer replacements coming through the ranks. There is also an increased demand for further training and reskilling for mature workers to stay in touch and succeed in the workforce.

Many people have realized the importance of systematic career management and self-development. The market currently wants people who have developed specialist skills rather than generalists, as companies now tend to focus more closely on their core business and outsource noncore or specialist work such as information technology, marketing, human resources, training, and logistics. This means that people in the job market with generalist skills such as general managers, retail managers, and bank branch managers are becoming less needed.

It is necessary for us to manage our careers and to build our skills. By developing our career, we will work and, hopefully, live longer.

Although many baby boomers recognize that retirement is years away, most are looking forward to it. Professor Thomas Muller of Griffith University, who specializes in "generation marketing", says the baby boomers were raised to believe that the world was their oyster, and after the triumphs of their easy and revolutionary youth, they found middle age disappointing. He says workplace demands and the desire to live middle-class lives has created great stress for baby boomers. "The baby boomers have succeeded economically but it has come at a huge cost." The costs include delaying marriage and childbearing, an increase in the number of divorces, alienation from their children, and the erosion of family values. "Baby boomers, by and large, have had a feeling that they have been on a perpetual treadmill," Muller says. Many see retirement as a chance to nurture themselves and their priorities will include enjoyment, self-fulfillment, giving something back to the community, and enhancing their knowledge and experiences.

Muller predicts that as the baby boomers age over the next 20 years, their activities will fall into eight key categories, including volunteering, spending time with grandchildren, education and travel. They will be driven by a desire to give something back, discover and learn. He says the baby boomers will also focus on spirituality and nostalgia, as they reflect on the past and search for meaning in their lives. But Muller agrees that baby boomers will age in a non traditional way; as a result, other trends will be entrepreneurialism—as the boomers try to remain busy and successful for the sake of enjoyment rather than financial necessity—and political activism, as they become leaders in the community for causes that affect them. . . .

The industries that are likely to expand as a result of ageing baby boomers include financial planning, entertainment, recreation and leisure, travel, restaurants, adult education, housing and all service industries.

Michelle Hannen, "Grey Revolutionaries,"
BRW (Australia), May 11, 2001.

Work should be mentally rewarding to everyone, no matter what their age. Career planning is now essential for older workers around the world to ensure they maintain a good quality of life throughout their mature years.

The increase in employment of older workers has highlighted a number of issues that need to be addressed, including these:

- Changes to performance management systems to make allowance for the career aspirations of older workers compared to those of younger workers
- Health and safety issues
- Strategies for managing older worker
- Opportunities for promotion for younger people
- Managing relationships between the older and younger generations
- Managing discrimination in recruitment
- Placing a value on the skills, experience, and knowledge that older workers have
- Training and development for older workers, including career planning in the new workplace
- Putting retirement processes in place
- Dealing with unemployment for older people who are less likely to have a government retirement fund
- Financial planning for workers generally

Globally, the number of older working people is astronomical. Corporations will continue to look to older workers to fill certain jobs, and the mature candidate pool will need to be technologically astute and flexible to tool up for the opportunities that may be available.

SUMMARY

There are now more choices and opportunities for us to live and work in different countries than ever before. It is beneficial for us to understand the various retirement practices, government intervention, influences, and assistance provided to retired and mature workers around the globe.

In most countries today, there is a trend to eliminate discrimination against older workers and design more suitable employment conditions. Attitudes and expectations toward older workers are gradually aligning with the reality of extended life expectancy and an improved quality of life for older workers.

• *Support for mature workers.* Many of us take for granted that our government will offer some support for us in retirement. Some countries, however, provide little or no government assistance to older workers; the assumption is that families will take care of these individuals in their later years. Whether the government in your country provides benefits or not, one message comes through loud and clear: we must all ensure the security of our futures with the help of planned savings or continued work, whether part time or full time.

• *Early and voluntary retirement plans.* As improved health and changing ideas allow many people to work far longer than in the past, early or voluntary retirement plans are growing more common. Such plans are usually developed in response to restructurings or mergers and acquisitions.

• *Understanding the worth of older workers.* There is an increasing awareness and appreciation of the continued worth of older workers. More governments and companies throughout the world are offering incentives for them to remain in the workforce.

• *Attitudes toward older workers.* Even as companies and governments work to keep older employees in the workforce, many individuals find they are still discriminated against in the workplace despite laws prohibiting such behavior. Older workers can often be prejudicially considered behind the times simply on the basis of age. Although younger workers usually respect the experience of older peers, they sometimes doubt their ability to be innovative or move quickly. Younger workers may also resent the "know-it-all" attitude of some older workers and question their reluctance to reach decisions quickly.

• *Taking on full- or part-time roles.* Part-time work, project, and volunteer assignments have appeal to retirees. Many retired workers who accepted early retirement have now realized that the money saved for retirement will

Rewired, Rehired, or Retired?

run out during their lifetime. Therefore, many are returning or looking to return to the workplace. Aside from economic and longevity factors is the life interest issue. There is a growing trend to entice mature workers back into the workplace because of their experience and knowledge. Many organizations employ older workers of retirement age to work on special projects such as strategic planning, sales, and finance.

- *Demographic trends.* The older population is projected to increase in most countries due to rapidly aging populations as well as declining birthrates. Improved health is also contributing to increased life expectancy.
- *The effect of extended life expectancy.* Due to extended life expectancy, many people who have planned carefully for retirement are concerned about outliving their savings and becoming a burden to their children. Because of this, there is a trend for retirees to return to work to augment their retirement benefits and involve themselves with meaningful activity.

Many people have realized that systematic career management and self-development is urgent. The market currently wants specialists rather than generalists; thus, people who have developed their career and have wide-ranging skills will have the opportunity to work longer if they wish to. There is now an increased demand for further training and reskilling for the mature worker.

Work should always be mentally rewarding. Career planning is now essential for older workers around the world to ensure they maintain a good quality of life throughout their lifetime.

CHAPTER 12

Retractable Retirement

Here's something you may not realize: retirement does not have to be forever. You are allowed to change your mind. You can return to the workforce if that is your choice for securing a better life or sustaining your quality of life. Granted, it may seem to be an extremely daunting thought, and, realistically, it may not be easy to reenter the workforce following a period of retirement. But with proper planning and goal setting and an awareness of what you will be returning to, it can be done. Ultimately, in fact, if going back to work is what you really want, it's not a question of "can," but an issue of "should."

RETIRE *(vb). To give up or to cause (a person) to give up his work, esp. on reaching a pensionable age. To go away as into seclusion, for recuperation. To recede or disappear.*

Collins Dictionary

WHY WE RETIRE

Retirement typically sounds like a great option for most people—a reward for a lifetime of hard work. It presents the opportunity to do all those things we've thought about over the years but perhaps haven't had the time or money to complete. The sticking point, however, is that even as we do the things we've dreamed about,

Happiness in the older years of your life, like happiness in every year of life, is a matter of choice. Your choice for yourself.

Harold Azine

many of us find ourselves confronted by a superabundance of free time. The worst-case scenario involves people who have been working diligently for forty years, show up late at their own retirement parties (because they've been busy tying up loose ends), and then wake up the next morning with no sense of direction and purpose. They had never taken the time to contemplate their options or plan for the future.

Questions about how to deal with retirement have only intensified as companies have encouraged people to take early retirement at sixty, fifty-five, or even fifty years old. That's a great way to reduce an organization's cost structure while creating advancement opportunities for promising younger people. And the individuals who are offered these packages see them as a wonderfully generous opportunity: a financial enticement and the opportunity to leave a job (which you may have disliked, or thought you did) and go have some fun.

Imagine the point of view of people who started their careers at age sixteen to twenty or so and worked within the same organization all their professional lives, mixing with a close set of colleagues over that time. It's possible for such a band to talk each other into believing that their work and their employer are unsatisfactory. The situation may not be that bad at all, but if they have nothing to compare it to, their perceptions may displace any sense of perspective. Now imagine that the company announces its intention to cut costs, offering an early retirement program as one method to achieve its goal.

"That's just another example of how everything has gone downhill," one colleague tells another. "Let's get out while the getting's still good."

The decision is made, the leap is taken, and as the old saying goes, "It may not be the jump that's so painful, it's the landing." In fact, it is absolutely imperative that we plan retirement so that we continue to remain active, with mental, social, and physical stimulation.

180

I once worked with a man who could always tell me the years, months, and days he had remaining until his retirement. Yet while retiring seemed to be his major goal in life and a force that kept him going, he never expressed any desire to undertake anything in particular once he was retired. I lost contact with him, but I still wonder at odd moments whatever happened to him.

Another man couldn't wait to replace the day-to-day stress of working life to play golf at every available moment. He retired as soon as he reached age fifty-five. Today, six years into retirement, he finds that he can't afford to play golf as regularly as he had hoped. Perhaps if he'd worked another five years, he might have put himself in the financial position to play golf every day until he was ninety. In fact, he has given up the game entirely and is totally focused on the burden of making his money last.

> *The average life expectancy once a person retires with nothing to do is 5.7 years: Use it or lose it!*
>
> Denis E. Waitley (1933–),
> American speaker, trainer, author

Many people have a mind-set in which retirement becomes their reward for working hard over the years. Finally, they reach the point in life where they can relax and occupy their time as they choose. Reality does not always match the dream.

Case Study: Think Carefully About Your Reasons for Retirement

Three years after Richard attended his retirement lunch (following thirty-five years with one company), he is now contemplating his future. Richard has realized that he's no longer having fun in his retirement. He looks back to his days of employment with fond memories. He misses his colleagues, whom he now sees only infrequently because they always seem to be busy.

When he was offered an early retirement package at age fifty-five, Richard leaped at the opportunity. He figured it was his reward for years of service to the organization. Finally, he and his wife would be able to fulfill their dream of moving to a beach community to live a peaceful existence.

They found a cottage near the water with an attached work shed where Richard decided he would devote more time to what had been a weekend hobby: wood turning. He was very talented and could make beautiful wooden items. The couple agreed that their new existence was a far cry from the busy lives they had led in their city home previously.

Richard now recognizes that their life has changed dramatically since retirement, and not necessarily for the better. Sure, they've gotten the opportunity to experience many things in a new environment. But Richard really misses his work associates, the everyday communication with clients, and the constant general interaction with new people. Their new home on the coast is located in an isolated area where they haven't made many new friends. Even the people they have made friends with don't seem to have a lot in common with them.

And although Richard's retirement package seemed attractive enough at the time, he and his wife are recognizing that they will be forced to adjust to a different standard of living.

Richard also now acknowledges that despite the fresh air and occasional walk along the beach, he has become more lethargic and overweight, and he doesn't cope as well with unpredictable pressures. He has found that little things that never used to bother him really irritate him. His life has become routine, and he is now questioning whether taking the early retirement package was such a good idea after all. Richard's wife also misses her friends and the busier lifestyle they had in the city.

Richard wonders whether it may be too late to change direction and return to employment. At fifty-eight years of age, he still feels extremely capable of taking on a job. He knows he needs the mental and social stimulation that returning to work will bring him. But how can he reenter the workforce?

Rewired, Rehired, or Retired?

Planning for Retirement

In planning for retirement, retirees need to plan what to do *after* they have retired. Consider the following list:

- Think of three things that you have always wanted to do and ask yourself, "Will I be able to do these things if I retire?"

- Ask your spouse or partner how she or he feels about your retiring and being at home more.

- Have you discussed your plans with your partner?

- Have you a circle of friends as well as hobbies, sports, and social activities that you will be able to expand on in retirement?

- Before retiring, talk to a reputable financial planner who can give you guidance as to whether your savings will be adequate to maintain the quality of life you want for you and your spouse or partner until you are age eighty-five.

(Continued)

Planning for Retirement (Continued)

- If you leave your job, can you work part time if you want or undertake alternative work?

- If you are serious about retiring and you have a choice, take one month's leave and live at home as if you have retired. See how you and your partner feel at the end of the month.

- What new skills would you like to learn if you had more time?

- Are you happy with your current fitness level?

- What plans do you have to maintain or improve your fitness level in retirement?

- Would you like to travel widely?

- Develop an action plan for the first year of retirement that will meet your personal needs. Discuss this plan with your partner and seek feedback.

Rewired, Rehired, or Retired?

CHALLENGES OF REENTERING THE WORKFORCE

There are many challenges to face when deciding to reenter the workforce after retirement. But however daunting or challenging that path may appear to be, it is certainly preferable to focus on a fulfilling, stimulating future rather than reflect on the past and live the rest of your life stuck in neutral, wondering what might have been.

Experience is not what happens to you. It is what you do with what happens to you.

Aldous Huxley (1894–1963),
British author

By identifying and confronting the developments and changes in the world of work since your retirement, you will be able to take on these challenges with knowledge and purpose, and gain confidence quickly.

New Technology

Consider the changes in technology that have occurred since you retired. Developments in everyday electronic communication may seem off-putting initially because you're not familiar with them. In fact, technology is becoming more and more user friendly.

The fact is that today, you have no choice but to be computer literate if you want to succeed, or even survive, in the workplace. Once, it was a matter of writing your message on a piece of paper and sending it to its destination using the fax machine. The fax seems to be used minimally these days. The ability to communicate by e-mail means the message gets to its destination virtually instantaneously. Cell phones, videoconferencing, data projector presentations, Internet conferencing, intranets, and other virtual office concepts have fundamentally changed the way we communicate these days. It is almost impossible to be unreachable.

You may, of course, already be extremely familiar with these new communication methods. But if you're not, don't worry. If you're prepared to invest time in a course or find an individual to teach you new skills, it is easy to get up to speed quickly with the latest gear.

There are plenty of "Introduction to Computers" courses available at adult education colleges. They're usually advertised in local newspapers and magazines. Otherwise, if you visit your local bookstore, you're bound to find a whole section of the store dedicated to books that will help you learn about computers and the latest in electronic communication. The hardest part when it comes to learning about computers is getting started, but from then on, you'll soon wonder how you ever got by without the latest technology.

Concept of Service

Just when we thought the world was heading toward shorter working hours, it seems we are rapidly evolving into a "24-7" way of work. More and more companies are offering around-the-clock service, and that has created an increased need for all of us to be flexible and adaptable to new working options and conditions.

In addition, more than ever before, companies are now focused on the fact that the customer is king. Competing in tough global markets, businesses are looking for an edge over competitors by offering the best possible service to their customers.

Of course, cost-cutting, budget-conscious businesses are the ones that have survived the competitive upheavals of recent business history. The trend has resulted in fewer employees working longer hours.

The Work Environment

The typical work environment has also changed dramatically in just a few years. There is a trend in many businesses to a more casual environment, where business suits may no longer be required and more casual attire is accepted.

Office furniture and equipment have changed. Fewer and fewer people have private offices. Struggling to attract and retain the best people, many companies now work hard to keep their employees happy by building health clubs and child care facilities on site, installing espresso machines in comfortable staff lounges, even providing concierge services so that employees can concentrate on their work and not worry whether they'll get to the dry cleaners before the store closes.

The Need to Adjust

After several retirement years of waking up when you feel like it and occupying your time each day with activities you have chosen, it will take some adjustment and discipline to fall back into a work routine. You may now have to take direction from a boss who is far younger than you (possibly the same age as your children). People may not show you the respect you believe you deserve. This may make you feel a lack of status compared to what you were used to in the past.

The reality is that, like it or not, you will need to address how you should behave in your new working environment. The environment will not conform to you; you must conform to it to work effectively.

STAYING IN TOUCH

We all know people in their seventies and eighties who are alert, wise, and respected for their experience and wisdom and who are full of energy, vitality, and an enthusiasm for life. We probably also know individuals of a similar age who have little to talk about, seem to complain regularly, have a negative attitude, and show little in the way of a healthy sense of humor. (There are also people who fit this description and are in their forties, fifties, or sixties.)

Often these individuals suffer from a lack of regular mental stimulation. Numerous medical studies support the theory that keeping yourself mentally (and physically) active will result in a better life for you.

If you are retired today but are thinking about reentering the workforce, it may make sense to focus your mental exercise program on issues or areas that will support your

> *The secret of success is constancy of purpose.*
>
> Benjamin Disraeli (1804–1881),
> British prime minister

return to the working world. Many people maintain business interests in retirement, for example, to keep in touch with current developments. Others spend time managing their own investment portfolios or retirement funds.

Keep abreast of accounting requirements and new tax issues. If you have an investment portfolio, research into different options can support your financial needs while keeping you attuned to changing business conditions. Investigate the technologies the companies you have invested in have adopted, for example. Determine whether and why their products and services will be applicable in the future. Make your own case regarding whether their performance will improve or deteriorate in the future. Canny investors gain considerable knowledge and business skills. The combination helps them understand the broader business world and identify the companies that will be successful tomorrow.

Life was meant to be lived and curiosity must be kept alive. One must never, for whatever reason, turn his back on life.

Eleanor Roosevelt (1884–1962),
American first lady,
lecturer, humanitarian

Being involved on a board or committee of a charitable organization or club can be another effective way to keep in touch. Attending meetings and interacting with other board or committee members, presenting reports, and understanding the initiatives being adopted or pursued by the organization will help you stay up to date.

When I started my consulting business, I found that I conducted the vast majority of my research and development activities while I was actively engaged in work for my clients. I was also a director on public company boards at the time, and those positions kept me aware of what was new and necessary from the perspective of a wide cross-section of businesses. It ensured that while I was operating as a consultant, I didn't lose touch with the larger business and economic picture.

CONSIDER PART-TIME WORK

As you contemplate your options and think about reentering the workforce, you may have a nagging sense that you don't want to go back to the rat race, working endless hours and reducing the leisure time you've grown used to.

It is better to wear out than to rust out.

Traditional saying

Outsourcing has created a range of new opportunities for people to work part time as contractors or consultants. The growth in this area of employment continues to increase around the world. The situation offers you an opportunity to reenter the workforce while maintaining the positive aspects of retirement you have come to enjoy.

Imagine a job that is enjoyable and stimulating, enables you to work two or three days a week, and provides you with additional income to support your lifestyle. At the same time, you retain adequate leisure time to pursue your nonwork priorities and, most important, have fun with your life. These jobs exist. Start thinking about the prospect of finding one if that route appeals to you.

> Pension plans that encourage early retirement, together with continuing age discrimination are at odds with people living longer, says the 33 million strong American Association of Retired Persons in its guide for employers. "This means large and growing costs to subsidize retirees, concurrent with a large and growing shortage of requisite skills. These trends do not add up and they are unsustainable."
>
> Alison Maitland, "The Benefits of Going Gradually," *Financial Times,* August 2, 2000.

SUMMARY

Retirement does not have to be forever. You are allowed to change your mind and return to the workforce. Although it may seem to be an extremely difficult process, it is achievable with proper planning, goal setting, and an awareness of what you will be returning to.

> *It is never too late to be what you might have been.*
>
> George Eliot (1819–1880),
> British novelist

- *Why we retire.* Retirement can provide you with the opportunity to do what you've always wanted to do but perhaps haven't had the time or money for previously. The most important thing to do to enjoy retirement is to give strong consideration to the future and the goals you would like to achieve. It is common for people to discover that retirement is not all they had anticipated. It is certainly preferable to make whatever changes are necessary to focus on a fulfilling and stimulating future rather than reflect on the past and live life in neutral.

- *Challenges of reentering the workforce.* Deciding to reenter the workforce requires a commitment to adapt to new challenges—for example, learning new technology, understanding a company's concept of service, becoming aware of the style of work environment, and adjusting your frame of mind to take direction from a boss once again.

- *Staying in touch.* Most people are able to maintain business interests in retirement that keep them in touch with current developments in the business world to ease the process of returning to the workplace should they choose to do so.

> *Retirement takes all the fun out of Saturdays.*
>
> Author unknown

- *Consider part-time work.* More and more companies are outsourcing services on a contract or consultancy basis. This creates abundant new opportunities to reenter the workforce while maintaining the positive aspects of retirement.

Rewired, Rehired, or Retired?

CHAPTER 13

Life Is Not a Dress Rehearsal

Your life is right now, so you must make the most of every moment and keep your dreams alive.

COMMIT YOURSELF TO HAVING A LIFE

Society attaches a number to us and expects us to think and behave like a person of that age. . . .

And we start to believe it.

"I would if I was younger; I'm too old to go back to school; It's too late for me to get in shape; I'm too old to find someone; Not at my age."

Rubbish!

Don't let age be a barrier. Do what you want, no matter how old you are.

You can marry at 40, take up sport at 50 and change careers at 60.

And you can keep dancing at 80.

Patrick William Moore, *Ways to Fly* (2000).

If you've reached, or are about to turn, fifty, you may be at a stage in your life where many significant responsibilities are now behind you. Perhaps you've paid off a mortgage and watched your children build lives and start careers of their own. (Mind you, there are more new parents in their forties today than ever before, so this may not necessarily be the case for everyone.)

If you've established a solid financial base for yourself over the years, this is a good time to begin thinking about how—and when—you may want to put it to good use.

Do you want to retire at age fifty-five? Would you rather keep working full time until you're seventy or older? Does the thought of a new career or a new job that lets you combine features of work and retirement appeal to you? Whatever your wishes may be, the sooner the better to begin thinking about how to use your time to attain maximum enjoyment and fulfillment throughout your mature years.

No matter how healthy or fit we are today, there's no way to tell how long we'll be around to enjoy what we've worked for. Will it be one, ten, twenty, thirty, or forty years? When is the magic day going to arrive when you start to realize that life is for living? When—if you're not already—are you going to do what you want with your time?

We've all heard the stories about people retiring, only to die a short time later, never getting to fulfill their retirement goals. So why wait for retirement? Start committing yourself to having a life from this very moment on. Ensure you are getting out of life all the things that make you happy.

It's easy to focus so strongly on the future that we keep working toward it without stopping to decide when the future actually starts for us. If we're stuck in this rut, getting out of it typically means agreeing to focus, and then act, on ways to achieve a more well-rounded work-life balance for ourselves. It's just too easy to keep old habits and never actually get to enjoy what we have worked so hard for. Life must be lived to the full *now*. There's no point in rehearsing for a future that may not happen.

Some people as they mature simply forget how to have fun. Frightening, isn't it? Unfortunately, it's true. I'm sure we can all think of people we've met who fit this model.

CHOICES FOR LIVING

Having—or getting—a life doesn't necessarily mean replacing work with full-time retirement, of course. What you need to do is commit yourself to determine what you get the most from in life. If you decide to give up work, what activities will provide you with enough stimulation and enjoyment to continue an active life?

If your work is exciting, gratifying, and rewarding and it's what you want to do most, then your answer is simple: keep working and enjoy your fulfilling life. Just be sure you constantly ask yourself along the way if this is the path you really want to lead at this stage of your life.

The years will wrinkle the skin, but to give up enthusiasm wrinkles the soul.

Author unknown

You could be focused on the collateral benefits that come from working: driving an expensive company car, perhaps, or living in a trophy house, traveling the world at the front of the plane instead of at the back, staying in luxury hotels, and so forth. If these are legitimately important to you, then they are valid reasons to keep working.

There are also intangible benefits that may make you choose to continue to work. You may feel that you're making a positive difference in the world, for example, or contributing to improving people's lives, pursuing exciting activities, and achieving great personal pride. Your job role may help you fulfill personal needs for power, status, and pride in the eyes of your family and friends. All of these can be valid reasons to continue working.

There are people who would do their jobs for far less pay than they actually receive because they love what they're doing so much. Why should they change? If you still love working, then why shouldn't you continue doing what you enjoy?

Time, like a snowflake, disappears while we're trying to decide what to do with it.

Author unknown

Case Study: Active Retirement Is Not Only Fun, It's Good for You!

Vern retired from his job with the Government Water and Irrigation Authority at the age of sixty-two. Throughout his working life, he had spent much of his spare time actively involved in a services club that provided amenities to disadvantaged people in the district where he lived, looked after widows of war veterans, and sponsored opportunities for younger people to gain skills through sports and other learning activities.

Because he was passionate about the club and how it helped the people in his community, Vern had a ready-made career alternative awaiting him at retirement. His involvement in the club gave him status in the community following his retirement and served his needs for contributing to the community. While his position was an honorary role for a nonprofit organization, his reward came from helping the enterprise grow into a significant commercial business, with its profits being used for the betterment of the lives of the people in the community.

By remaining active in his community, he continued to be intellectually alert, maintained his close business friends and associates, and lived life to the full and had fun. In fact, until his death at the age of seventy-seven, he was involved in the club's day-to-day activities as a director. He worked the hours that suited him and also reserved time for leisure activities. Although he experienced significant ill health during the last decade of his life, he continued to look forward to and participate actively in the club.

Those closest to him agreed that his involvement in the club and passion and dedication to the community added at least an extra five years to his life.

Live not as though there were a thousand years ahead of you. Fate is at your elbow; make yourself good while life and power are still yours.

Marcus Aurelius (A.D. 121–180),
Roman emperor, philosopher

WHERE ARE YOU NOW?

Not all of us have fantastic jobs that we want to continue doing forever. For some of us, our job is routine, boring, and lacking in excitement and does not yield the tangible and intangible benefits we need for a happy life.

If that's your position, it's time to do something about it. Perhaps you should stop building up an inheri-

Rewired, Rehired, or Retired?

tance for your children, recognize that you have saved enough to enjoy a good standard of living, and decide that it's time to get out there and enjoy it. The key here is to consider and plan carefully how you are going to enjoy yourself. Active retirement is a good way to live a stimulating and exciting life that can enable you to take on new challenges.

Live every day as if it were your last. Do every job as if you were the boss. Drive as if all other vehicles were police cars. Treat everybody else as if he were you.

Phoenix Flame

ACTIVE RETIREMENT AND LIVING

Be honest with yourself about your values and goals, strengths and weaknesses, needs and objectives. Then try to align them with future opportunities and realities. Identify what your motivation in life is, and make sure your plan encompasses these needs. Do you desire status, creativity, social contact, physical or mental stimulation, adventure, or more money? Many of the social and emotional rewards previously provided at work can also come from purposeful activities in retirement.

Case Study: Retirement Doesn't Have to Slow You Down

Seventy-nine-year-old Ted was president of a major international corporation when he retired in his early sixties. Since then, he has maintained his business interests through active and passive investments. He is proficient with computers and is able to relate well with older and younger people alike.

Ted and his wife, Rosemary, divide their time between Colorado, Florida, and world travel, spending one-third of the year in Colorado, where they enjoy skiing, golf, and bike riding, and the remainder in Florida or on one of their frequent trips abroad. They are both extremely active people who are mentally alert and fun to be with. Ted has clearly focused on active retirement and is now living his life to the full and having fun.

Purposeful activity provides significantly higher levels of satisfaction with lower levels of depression and stress than inactivity. It's a strong component of a well-balanced and happy retirement.

The list of challenges you can set yourself to enjoy is endless if you have a positive attitude (and many don't cost a lot of money)—for example:

- Volunteer work or helping others
- Creative hobbies
- Undertaking studies and learning new skills
- Becoming an active member of a club
- Part-time work in a low-stress environment
- Starting a small business
- Maintaining fitness
- Travel
- Athletic interests aligned with your physical capacity
- Reading

Nothing is really work unless you would rather be doing something else.

Author unknown

I know someone who in retirement decided to build rocking horses for his grandchildren. These rocking horses were built with much love and care and were of an extremely high quality—so much so that it didn't take long for friends of the family to notice these beautiful treasures and order rocking horses to be made for them. He is now producing rocking horses commercially, which has developed into an extremely profitable business for him. He gets to spend his time doing what he loves and gets paid for it.

Doing something that is exciting, extraordinary, creative, or stimulating is not just for the rich and famous. Why can't we spend our time doing something we love? All of us were born special, so let's not forget it!

Those who are athletic can strive to compete in the Masters Games, the equivalent to the Olympic Games for the senior age group. If you enjoy a particular sport, imagine representing your country in the Masters. It could be a dream come true. What's stopping you? Start training now. You may not make the team, but you'll have a lot of fun trying. Just think how fit you'll be.

To determine your own list of priorities, find a relaxing place, close your eyes, and imagine you have the perfect life. Look around you. Where are you? Who's with you? What are you doing? How do you feel? Open your eyes when you have finished indulging in this vision. Can you make that vision a reality?

The range of options available to you is virtually unlimited, so determine what interests you the most. How can you prepare to take on these activities, what financial requirements may apply, and who else will be involved?

HAPPINESS HURDLES

As you work to achieve the goal of having a happy life throughout your mature years, watch out for traps that can get in the way of the future you wish for. Here are some observations that are applicable to both those who remain active in the workforce and those who pursue an active retirement:

- If you cannot resolve pain experienced after a forced retirement, you may never be able to move forward optimistically. Address such issues. Don't let psychological stress hold you back from achieving new life goals. You can't change what has already happened.

- Don't leave retirement too late. Make sure you still have the energy and enthusiasm for life to fulfill your goals and enjoy your mature years.

You can't do good if you don't feel good.

Denis E. Waitley (1933–),
American speaker, trainer, author

Vision of Retirement.

Write out, in your own words, your vision of how you would like your retirement to be.

- Don't retire without a plan. Careful planning prior to retirement can make the transition—and the rest of your life—far smoother.

- Ensure that your perception of retirement is based on reality, not just a way of escaping from an unrewarding job.

- Make certain that you will be financially positioned to fulfill your life's dreams and goals into the future. Will you have to rely on a fixed pension, or will you enjoy financial independence to pursue desired activities in the years to come?

- Make sure you have a healthy amount of social contact daily or weekly. Social isolation is not good. Once you're removed from the daily give and take of the workplace, the need for social interaction is heightened.

- Find ways to have a sense of belonging and contribution to society. Voluntary work is a great way to achieve this.

- Make sure life continues to have variety and purpose. What good will come from lying around the house doing nothing all day?

> *Happiness is not a goal but what you feel on the way to achieving your goal.*
>
> Author unknown

- Keep yourself well. Make a serious commitment to exercise regularly and stick to a healthy diet to eliminate high levels of emotional stress, laziness, and illness or disease.

- Remember that change is constant. Remain adaptable along the way, understanding that you may need to change or fine-tune your plans in the future.

- Be proud of your own skills and abilities. People spend too much time dwelling on past events or dreaming about what might happen in the future. It doesn't bring you any closer to achieving your goals.

- It is easy to become resentful and critical of others who are successful and have done something useful with their lives. Don't fall into this trap.

DON'T WAIT FOR LIFE TO COME TO YOU

Many of us insist on living in a fantasy world, thinking that if we wait patiently, something will magically appear in our lives to reward us with the future we've always longed for. Stop dreaming of winning the lottery or meeting generous millionaires who will take care of all your wants and needs for the future. Do something for yourself.

Case Study: An Ongoing Search for New Challenges and Goals Can Make a Difference

John jumped at the opportunity to retire on reaching the age of fifty-five when it was offered to him after serving forty years with the local hardware business in the country town he lives in.

For many years, John had complained that the work he was doing was boring, but he decided to stay with the company because he believed there was no alternative. There were no other opportunities for someone of his age within the town, and he wasn't prepared to travel an hour each way to work in the large city nearby. At his age, he believed it was far too difficult to learn new skills.

Over the next few years, John continued to believe he was lucky, not having to work any more. His time was his own, so he could sleep in until midday if he chose to. He didn't involve himself in any community activities and thought the best way to use his time was to try and relax and have a drink with friends.

John recently celebrated his sixtieth birthday at a luncheon in the town attended by his family and friends. The party started on time at noon. What was unusual was that there was virtually no laughing and very little interaction among people. No one got up to make speeches and tell funny stories about John. Soon the people got up from their seats and went home. What should have been a celebration of sixty years of life and a wonderful time for the guest of honor and his guests was unmemorable.

In fact, most of the people at the party were in a situation similar to John's. Many had taken early retirement and had chosen to do little within their community. Their brains seem to have slowed down. Gone were their energy, excitement about life, sense of humor, and zest for living. It was as if everyone had given up on living.

John and his friends had taken the option to drop out of working life. That in itself is fine. But they have never replaced work with new challenges in their lives. A lot of their general discussion now revolves around negative issues: reports of new sickness and prophecies of doom and gloom.

Regrettably, John and his friends have now let precious years of their lives disappear. They have missed out on what could have been a wonderful and rewarding time.

SUMMARY

The person who controls your future is you. What do you want to do? Why aren't you doing it now? What's stopping you?

- *Commit yourself to having a life.* If you have worked hard all your life and have built up a reserve fund for your advancing years, when do you plan to put it all to good use? Start committing yourself to having a life from this moment on. There's no point in rehearsing for a future that may not happen.
- *Choices for living.* You can keep working and enjoy a fulfilling life if the work you do is not only an exciting, gratifying, and rewarding experience but also what you want to do most. Ask yourself constantly if this is the path you really want to lead at this stage of your life.

We become what we think of most of the time; winners dwell on the rewards of success, losers dwell on the consequences of failure.

It doesn't matter what happens in life, it's how you react to it.

Denis E. Waitley (1933–),
American speaker, trainer, author

- *Where are you now?* It may be time to get out and enjoy your life. Just be sure to consider and plan how you are going to enjoy yourself.
- *Active retirement and living.* Many of the social and emotional rewards previously provided at work can also come from purposeful activities in retirement. Ask yourself which activities interest you the most, how you can prepare to take on these activities, what the financial requirements are, and who else will be involved in these activities.
- *Happiness hurdles.* Although your goal is to have a happy life throughout your mature years, be aware of, and avoid, the many traps that can potentially be damaging to the future you wish for.
- *Don't wait for life to come to you.* Ultimately, you're the only one who can make your dreams come true. Don't wait for someone else to step in as your guardian angel. Act for yourself.

A FINAL NOTE FROM THE AUTHOR

I hope you have found the suggestions in this book of value. Perhaps you can now use the book as a living guide for reviewing your plans regularly and developing action strategies for the future.

Remember to consider your personal needs and values. Clarity for the future comes from research, self-examination, honesty, and planning. Whether you choose to continue full- or part-time work or an active retirement, be sure you are going to enjoy your life. It is exciting to acknowledge that by your own thoughts and actions you can create the future you've always wanted.

You are responsible for what happens to you throughout your lifetime so what are you waiting for? Embrace your future, step forward bravely along the road you choose, and be the best you can.

BIBLIOGRAPHY

American Association of Retired Persons. (1998). *American business and older employees.* Washington, DC.

American Association of Retired Persons. (2001, May). *Beyond 50: A report to the nation on economic security.* Washington, DC.

Anderson, H. (2001, January 27). France finds time for the good life. *Weekend Australian,* p. 20.

Bridges, W. (1995). *Managing transitions: Making the most of change.* Cambridge, MA: Perseus/London: Nicholas Brealey.

Butler, R. (2000, August). *How we live as long as we live.* New York: American Museum of Natural History. www. amnh.org.

Cabinet Office, Performance and Innovation Unit, UK. (2000, April). *Winning the generation game. Chapter 6—The case for age discrimination legislation.* www.cabinet-office.gov.uk.

Christmas, L. (2001, January 27). Knock off time. *Weekend Australian.* pp. 17, 21.

Computer Economics. (1999, January). www.commerce.net.

Coursey, D. (2000, November 8). Experience counts: Revenge of the old guys. *ZDNet News.*

Drake Beam Morin, Inc. (2001, April). *CEO turnover & job security.*

Drake Beam Morin, Inc. (2001, April). *Realities of the executive job search.*

Drake Beam Morin, Inc. (2001, September). *Career choices and challenges of younger & older workers.*

Drucker, P. (1995). *Managing in a time of great change.* New York: Butterworth-Heinemann.

Dudley, G.W., & Goodson, S.L. (1999). *The psychology of sales call reluctance: Earning what you're worth in sales.* Dallas, TX: Behavioral Sciences Research Press.

Dychtwald, K. (1999). *Age power.* New York: Jeremy P. Tarcher, a division of Penguin Putnam Inc.

Hannen, M. (2001, May 11). *Grey revolutionaries.* BRW. Australia. pp. 64–67.

Howarth, B. (2001, July 13). *The outside experts.* BRW. Australia. p. 61.

Insec. (2000). La France En Fails et Chiffnes. *Population.* www.insec.com.

Intelliquest. (1999, April 27). *83 million US adults online.* www.nua.com.

KFC. (2001) *About KFC—The story of Colonel Harland Sanders.* www.kfc.com.

Macken, J. (2000, July 11). Finished at 45. *Australian Financial Review,* p. 50.

Maitland, A. (2000, August 2). The benefits of going gradually. *Financial Times,* p. 21.

Mansfield, P. (1994). *Why am I afraid to be assertive.* London: HarperCollins.

Mergerstat. (2001). *M & A activity report.* Los Angeles, CA: Author. www. mergerstat. com.

Moore, P.W. (2000). *Ways to fly.* McMahons Point, Australia: Way Books.

Patrickson, M. (1999, March). *Valuing the older worker conference,* Human Rights Commission, Auckland, New Zealand.

Peck, M.S. (1990). *The road less traveled.* New York: Simon & Schuster/London: Blake Friedmann Literary Agency.

Ridderstråle, J., & Nordström, K. (2000). *Funky business.* Stockholm, Sweden: BookHouse Publishing.

South African Government Statistical Services (2001). www.statssa.gov.co.za.

Sparrow, M. (1999, March). *Valuing the older worker conference,* Human Rights Commission, Auckland, New Zealand.

Statistics Canada. (2001) *The Daily*—Population Projections 2000–2026. www.statcan.ca.

Thomson Financial Services. (2001). *Merger and acquisition figures.* New York.

U.S. Bureau of Labor Statistics & Bureau of the Census. (2001). Current Population survey. www.bls.gov.

Walsh, M.W. (2001, April 15). No time to put your feet up as retirement comes in stages. *New York Times.*

Watson Wyatt Worldwide. (1995). *Best practice in corporate restructuring.* Washington, DC.

West, L.A., & Kinsella, K. (1997, May). Pension management and reform in Asia: An overview. *NBR Executive Insight, 11.* Seattle, WA: The National Bureau of Asian Research.

Young company, old worker. (2000, September 12). *Fortune,* Small Business Edition. Time Inc.

THE AUTHOR

Robert Critchley grew up in Strathalbyn, South Australia, where he joined the local branch of a large international bank. His career in banking covered all aspects of banking and finance while living in Australia and the United Kingdom, as well as working on assignments in the United States, Asia, and Europe.

Stepping out from the shelter and perceived security of banking at the age of forty-two, he built a successful consulting practice specializing in corporate recoveries, strategic planning, and training. In conjunction with his colleagues, he also established an outplacement and career transition business in Australia under license from Drake Beam Morin, the worldwide industry leader.

After developing the outplacement and career transition business and selling it to DBM, he has served in many leading senior executive roles overseeing DBM's international operations around the world. He also holds external directorships with publicly listed companies.

Critchley works closely with organizations undergoing restructuring and individuals affected by job loss and career change. An expert with a passion for improving people's lives and helping them to achieve maximum career satisfaction, he is regularly sought out by both the print and broadcast media worldwide to provide insightful commentary and advice. For more information visit the author's web site on *www.robertcritchley.com*.

INDEX

Avaya, 166, 167
Azine, H., 180

B

Baby boomer generation, 38, 167; changes in lifetime of, 53–54; demographic trends and, 169–171, 177; expectations of, 173–174; extended life expectancy and, 171–175, 177. *See also* Mature workers

Balance in work and life. *See* Work-life balance

Bankers, 59–60, 72–73

Banking industry, 64; consolidation in, 32, 65

Being yourself, 64–65, 68

Belgium, incentives to mature workers in, 163–164

Bell, A. G., 112

Bell, J. A., 62

"Benefits of Going Gradually, The," 189

Best Employer list, 12

"Best fit" assessment, 149

Bhutto, B., 132

Board membership, 188

Body language, 75, 77, 94

Boeing Corporation, 62

Bonne Bell, 62

Boredom: retirement and, 9, 16; as stressor, 7, 16, 19

BP, 162

B&Q hardware chain, 70, 72

Brain capacity, 72

Brain drain, 169

Bridges, W., 33–34

Britain. *See* United Kingdom

Buffett, W., 62

Burnett, L., 121

Business owners, local, 119

Business Review Weekly, 173–174

Business Week, 57

Butler, R., 4

C

Camus, A., 35

"Can do" factors, 149

Canada: aging population in, 169; incentives to mature workers in, 163, 168, 170; retirement age in, 160

Candidate assessment factors, 149

Career, current: assessing achievements in, 45; assessing level of interaction in, 46; assessing responsibilities and pressures in, 45–46; assessing satisfiers and dissatisfiers of, 42–44, 51–52; continuing, as choice, 3–4; tangible and intangible benefits of, 193. *See also* Job, current

Career, new: as a choice, 4; global opportunities for, 159–177; myths about mature workers and, 60–62, 69–70; self-assessment for, 48. *See also* Job, new; Job search

Career as personal responsibility: after job loss, 112, 114; global trends and, 173–175; lack of preparation for, 23; workplace trends toward, 10, 23, 27–29

Career ladder, 26–27

Career lattice, 26–27

Career planning, 174–175

Carnevale, 36

Carter, J., 62

Casual dress, 56, 79–80, 186

Change, personal: embracing, 38–39, 40, 199; misconceptions about, 37–38; organizational change process and, 34–35, 37–38, 40; reactions to, 32–35, 39–40; resistance to, 111–112, 114, 125; three-phase model of, 33–34

Change and trends, 21–40; affecting reentry to workforce, 185–187; global demographic, 169–171, 177; globalization and, 10, 31, 159–161; history of, 22–24, 39; importance of adaptability to, 56–58; increased pace of, 21, 22, 51; individual responses to, 32–35, 39–40, 125; job security and, 10, 22–24, 27–28; listed, 24–25; mature workers and, 159–161, 169–175; misconceptions about, 37–38; networking and, 115, 116; organizational process of, 34–38, 40; reasons for, 29–32, 39; in retirement and pension plans, 161–163,

F

Face-to-face meeting, 148–150, 156. *See also* Interviews

Failure, fear of, 126, 131

Family: assessing the needs of, 47–48; impact of retirement on, 17, 19; job loss and, 102–105, 113; as network contacts, 119; for telephone call prospecting, 132, 137

Favors, trading, 116

Faxes, 145, 185

Fear: of failure and rejection, 126, 131; of the unknown, 130–131. *See also* Phone phobia

Feeler communication style: characteristics of, 87; communicating with, 90, 91, 92; defined, 86; signs of, 90

Fifty-year-olds, 191–192

Financial status and needs: company-sponsored retirement plans and, 162–163; government-sponsored benefits and, 161–162; job loss and, 106; job search and, 154, 155; retirement decision and, 8–9, 18, 199

Financial Times, 189

"Finished at 45," 99

Finland: early retirement plans in, 163; mature workers in, 170

Fit: cultural, 45, 56, 80, 149; of job opportunity to personal goals, 78, 83, 154–155

Fitness. *See* Health and fitness

Flame, P., 195

Flattened organization, 31

Flexibility, 36, 38, 66, 69; exercising, 59–60, 68; importance of, 56–58; self-assessment of, 68

Follow-up, 145–148; e-mail, 145–147; telephone call, 147–148

Fortune Small Business Edition, 63

Fosdick, H. E., 18

France: incentives to mature workers in, 163–164; mature workers in, 170; 35-hour work week in, 15–16

Franklin, B., 116

Free time, 180

Friends: as network contacts, 119; support from, after job loss, 102–104, 113; for telephone call prospecting, 132, 137

Future, the: choices for, 2–7, 192–194; focusing on, with positive thinking, 109–110, 135, 137; self-assessment for, 41–52; starting today with, 1–3, 18, 191–192, 200, 202; taking a day to think about, 41–42, 51; work-life balance in, 1–19

G

Gatekeepers, tactics for getting the cooperation of, 143–145, 156

General Electric, 62

Generalists, 173

Generation marketing, 173–174

George, D. L., 124

Germany, history of retirement age in, 160

Giblin, F. J., II, 149

Glenn, J., 62

Global opportunities, 159–177; attitudes toward older workers and, 164–165; company retirement plans and, 162–163, 176; demographic trends and, 169–171, 177; extended life expectancy and, 171–175, 177; government-sponsored pension plans and, 161–162, 165–166, 176; for part-time work, 165–169, 176–177; summary points about, 175–177; work-life balance and, 165–169

Globalization trends, 10, 31, 159, 186

Goal setting: for interviews, 139–141, 156; for telephone calls, 132, 133

Goals: aligning job search with, 78, 83, 154–155; assessment of personal and career, 49–50; mature workers' ability to achieve, 51; retirement plan based on, 14–15, 180–184

Golden parachute, 162–163

Golfing, 14–15, 81

Goodson, S. L., 135

Government-sponsored pension plans, 161–162, 165–166, 176
"Grey Revolutionaries," 173–174
Grieving, 32, 33
Griffith University, 173–174
Griffiths, T., 166
Grooming, 79
Guidance, 48

H

Half, R., 74
Hannen, M., 173–174
Hansen, G., 17
Happiness: in active retirement, 191–202; hurdles to, 197–199, 202; in mature years, 191–202; in retirement, 179–182
"Having a job" *versus* "doing work," 25
Health and fitness: activity and, 17; choices and, 4, 7, 18; maintaining and improving, 18, 199; personal presentation and, 79, 149; self-assessment of, 48; for self-esteem after job loss, 106–107, 113; stress and, 7, 199
Hepburn, K., 137
Heraclitus, 23
Hewitt Associates, Best Companies to Work for in Australia, 12
Hobbies: in active retirement, 196; self-assessment of, 49
Hoffer, E., 56
Honesty, about experience and qualifications, 65–66, 68, 150
Hong Kong: aging population in, 171; early retirement plans in, 163; mature workers in, 168, 170; pension benefits in, 162
Howard, D. C., 167
Howarth, B., 31
Human resources, as organizational assets, 35–37, 40
Hunting and gathering age, 22
Hurdles to happiness, 197–199, 202
Huxley, A., 185

I

Iacocca, L., 62
"I-can-work-longer-than-you" fad, 11

ICI, 162
Incentives to mature workers, internationally, 163–169; demographic trends and, 169–171, 177
Industrial age, 22
Industries, transferring skills between, 64–65, 68
Industry consolidation, trend toward, 32, 65
Influence *versus* authority, 27
Information age, 22; mature workers adaptability in, 56–58; workplace change and, 30–31. *See also* Change and trends; Technology
Initial contact, 143–148; dealing with gatekeepers and, 143–145, 156; follow-up to, 145–148; overcoming phone phobia for, 125–138. *See also* Interviews; Telephone calls
Institute of Employment Research, Warwick University, 70, 72
Intellectual ability, 60, 72; mental stimulation and, 187–188
Interaction with others: assessing level of, in current career, 46; need for, 16–17, 19, 199; staying in touch with business trends and, 187–188
Interests, self-assessment of, 41–52
International Year of Older Persons, 159
Internet: globalization and, 159; researching prospective employers on, 73–74, 141–142
Interviews, job, 139–157; asking the right questions in, 151–152; communication guidelines for, 75–77, 148–152, 156–157; communication styles and, 86–92; company research prior to, 73–74, 83, 141–143, 156; conduct of, 148–152, 156–157; dimensions assessed in, 149–150; focusing on personal goals during, 78, 83, 154–155; follow-up to, 145–148; gatekeepers of, relating with, 143–145, 156; goal setting for, 139–141, 156; identifying decision influencers and decision makers for, 152–154, 157; interviewers who are too eager in, 154–155; listening in,

85–86, 93–94, 95, 150–152; literature about, 139; maximum goals for, 140–141; minimum goals for, 140; physical appearance for, 79–80, 83; positive attitude for, 75–77, 83; rehearsing, 74, 83; responding to questions in, 76–77, 151; sales meetings and, 139; setting up, 143–145; summary points for, 156–157; 10/50 rule for, 150–152, 156–157

"Introduction to Computers" courses, 186

Intuitor communication style: characteristics of, 87; communicating with, 91, 92; defined, 86; signs of, 90

Investment management, 188

Investor demands, 10, 11

I-SPEAK Your Language system, 86–95, 151; assessment of others with, 87, 90, 95; communication using, 90–92, 95; example of using, 92; personality styles in, 86–87; self-assessment with, 88–89, 94–95; summary points about, 94–95; value of, 91

Italy, aging population of, 7, 170

J

Japan: aging population of, 7, 169, 170, 171, 172; early retirement plans in, 163; end of lifelong employment in, 10; incentives to mature workers in, 164; personal computer use in, 57; retirement age in, 160; seniority system in, 172

Job, current: assessing satisfiers and dissatisfiers of, 42–44, 51–52; tangible and intangible benefits of, 193. *See also* Career, current

Job, having a, *versus* "doing work," 25

Job, new: aligning, with personal goals and interests, 78, 83, 154–155; global opportunities for, 159–177; mature workers in, 53–68; percentage of persons who obtain, through networking, 117; perception that mature workers can't get, 60–62, 68. *See also* Career, new; Job search

Job longevity, flexibility and, 59–60

Job loss, 97–114; communication of attitude about, 75; concerns presented by, 98; family and, 102–105, 113; mortality and, 99; nonprofit work after, 107–108, 113; organizational change and, 35–37, 40; positive thinking after, 108–110, 113–114, 197; precursors to, 38; reactions to, 32–35, 39–40, 97–100, 197; reality check after, 97–100, 112; resistance to change and, 111–112, 114; self-esteem rebuilding after, 98, 100, 101–114; summary points about, 112–113; trauma of, 97–100, 105, 112, 197; workplace trends and, 10, 11–12, 23, 30

Job search: aligning personal goals with, 78, 83, 154–155; dealing with recruiting and search firms in, 80–82, 83; decision influencers and decision makers in, 152–154, 157; networking for, 115–124; persistence in, 80–81, 145–148, 156; phone phobia and, 125–138; positive attitude for, 75–77, 83, 100, 108–111, 113–114; researching prospective employers for, 73–74, 83, 141–143, 156; summary points for, 82–83; using experience as an advantage during, 69–83; work-life balance goals and, 78. *See also* Interviews; Networking; Telephone calls

Job security: job loss realities and, 97; self-commitment and, 27–28; workplace change and loss of, 10, 22–24, 27–28

Job specifications, flexibility in, 81–82

Job titles, 27

Josepin, L., 15–16

Jung, C., 86

K

Keller, H., 97, 134

KFC, 66

Kinsella, K., 7, 170–171, 172–173

Korea: aging population in, 171; attitudes toward older workers in, 165, 166; retirement age in, 160

L

Latin America, pension privatization in, 161
Law firms, work-life balance in, 11–12
Leadership, old *versus* new paradigms of, 27
Learning, from mistakes, 72–73
Letters, 135, 147
Letting go, 14
Life expectancy: effect of extended, on global opportunities, 171–175, 177; increase in, 4, 7, 38, 160, 163; job loss and, 99; retirement decision and, 8
Lifelong employment: retirement after, 180; workplace change and loss of, 10, 22–24, 97
Link, H. C., 131
Listening, 78–79, 83, 85–86; active, 93–94, 95; in interviews, 85–86, 93–94, 95, 150–152; techniques of, 93–94; in telephone calls, 134; 10/50 rule for, 150–152, 156–157
"Little Protection for Older Workers," 72
Living: active retirement and, 195–198, 202; choices for, 192–194, 201; committing to, 191–192, 201; enjoyment of, 191–202; summary points for, 201–202
Lockheed Martin, 166
Losing streaks, 108–109
Loss, reactions to, 32–35, 97–100, 197. *See also* Job loss
Loyalty: job loss and, 97; traditional norm of, 22–23, 27–28

M

Macken, J., 99
Maitland, A., 14, 189
Management: flattening of layers of, 31; hiring of, 63; reactions of, to organizational change, 35. *See also* Chief executive officers
Managing Transitions (Bridges), 33–34
Mandatory retirement age, 160
Mandatory retirement contributions, 161

Mansfield, P., 76
Marden, O. S., 102
Marks & Spencer, 162
Mary Kay Cosmetics, 99
Masters Games, 197
Mature workers, 53–68; ability of, to achieve goals, 51; changes during the lifetimes of, 53–54; communication strategies for, 58; companies that value and hire, 62, 70, 72, 163–164; employability of, 60–62, 68, 69–72; employers' attitudes toward, 61; employers' attitudes towards, international comparison of, 164–165; flexibility in, 56–60, 66; global demographics of, 169–175, 177; global opportunities for, 159–177; impact of downsizing on, 35–37; incentives offered to, international comparison of, 163–169; issues of, 175; level playing field for, achieving a, 69–83; organizational change and, 35–37, 40; performance ability of, 60–62, 69–72; realities and myths of, 53–68, 69–70; search firms' attitudes toward, 80–82, 83; summary points about, 66–68; technology and, 56–58, 68; value of, to organizations, 35, 54–55, 58, 62, 63–64, 68, 163–164, 176; value of, to smaller companies, 63–64, 68; who have worked with one company, 59–60; who have worked within one industry, 64–65. *See also* Experience
May, P., 12
Mental stimulation, 187–188
Mercer, William M., 167–168
Mergers and acquisitions: industry consolidation and, 32, 65; trend toward, 10, 30
Middle managers, reactions of, to organizational change, 35
Mistakes, learning from, 72–73
Monsanto, 166, 167
Moore, P. W., 191

interviews, 143–145; thinking about the worst that could happen in, 130–131, 137; tips for making successful, 132–138; value of, 135, 137. *See also* Phone phobia

Temporary work: as option, 17; phased retirement and, 166; trend toward outsourcing and, 31–32

10/50 rule, 150–152, 156–157

Thailand: attitudes toward older workers in, 164; government support in, 162

Thibault, J.-A.F., 98

Thinker communication style: characteristics of, 87; communicating with, 91, 92; defined, 86; signs of, 90

Thinking positive, 108–110, 113–114, 196; for phone calls, 134, 135, 137, 138. *See also* Positive attitude

35-hour workweek, 15–16

Thomas, H., 62

Thoreau, H. D., 106

Tiredness, 18

Toffler, A., 57

Training, technology, 57–58, 185–186

Transfer of skills, between industries, 64–65, 68

Transfers, traditional norm of, 21–22

Transitions model, 33–34

Trauma, of job loss, 97–100, 105, 112

Travel, self-assessment of, 49

Travelers Insurance, 62

Treaty of Amsterdam, 1997, 165

Trends. *See* Change and trends

Turner, F., 2–3

Turnover: among older *versus* younger workers, 70, 72; of chief executive officers, 23–24; costs of, 36

U

United Kingdom: attitudes toward older workers in, 165; mature workers in, 70, 172; pension plans in, 162

United States: aging population in, 160–161, 171; incentives to mature workers in, 163, 165; personal computer use in, 57; retirement age in, 160, 163

U. S. Bureau of Labor Statistics, 171

Universities, phased retirement in, 166

University of Southern Queensland, 30

Unknown, fear of, 130–131

V

Virtual work space, 25–26

Visualization, 45, 133, 148, 197, 198

Vita Needle Company, 62

Voluntary retirement plans, 162–163, 176

Volunteer or service work, 165, 172, 194, 199. *See also* Nonprofit work

Von Bismarck, O., 160

W

Waitley, D. E., 181, 197, 201

Walking, 107

Walsh, M. W., 168

Walters, B., 62

Wardrobe, 56, 79–80, 186

Watson Wyatt, 29

Web sites, researching prospective employers on, 73–74, 141–142

West, L., 7, 170–171, 172–173

Western Europe: aging population of, 7; pension privatization in, 161

"Will do" factors, 149

William M. Mercer, 167–168

Winner, thinking like a, 108–110, 113–114

Work colleagues, as network contacts, 118

Work hours, value of shorter, 15–16

Work satisfiers and dissatisfiers, 42–44, 51–52. *See also* Satisfiers

Work style: in agrarian age, 22; change in, 21–40; in hunting and gathering age, 22; in industrial age, 22; in information age, 22

Work week, shorter, in France, 15–16

Workaholism: historical trends in, 11–13; workaphilism *versus*, 3, 13; work-life balance and, 11–14